To Lance Taylor with
appreciation and admiration.

Andrés Solimano
October 2012

Chile and the Neoliberal Trap

This book analyzes Chile's political economy over the past thirty years and its attempt to build a market society in a highly inegalitarian country, even though it is a new member of the Organization for Economic Cooperation and Development (OECD). This book provides a historical and contemporary background to Chile's economy and society, and discusses the cultural and institutional underpinnings of the imposition of a market society in authoritarian conditions in the 1970s and 1980s, and its maintenance in democracy in the 1990s and 2000s, as well as the counterreactions, mainly by social movements, to these attempts. Macroeconomic and growth policies and performance of the 1990s and 2000s are analyzed along with the record of poverty, inequality, and middle-class squeeze in the framework of social policies conducted under the privatization of education, health, and social security. The book documents the growing concentration of economic power (ownership, market shares, and productive structures) among small elites and discusses the evolution and limits of the democratic system built after the departure of the Pinochet regime.

Andrés Solimano is founder and chairman of the International Center for Globalization and Development in Santiago, Chile. He holds a PhD in economics from the Massachusetts Institute of Technology. Dr. Solimano was regional adviser at the United Nations Economic Commission for Latin America and the Caribbean, country director at the World Bank, executive director at the Inter-American Development Bank, and director of the Latin American School of Social Sciences in Chile. He was also director of the project on International Mobility of Talent with the United Nations University–World Institute of Economic Research and served as executive director for Chile on the board of the Inter-American Development Bank. Dr. Solimano has written extensively on international migration, talent mobility, growth, inequality, political economy, macroeconomics, and international development. His latest book is *International Migration in the Age of Crisis and Globalization* (Cambridge University Press, 2010).

To the memory of Alice Amsden, great friend and perceptive economist who left us too early.

To my family members, Bernardita, Gracia, Pedro and Paula.

To my father Ivan and late mother Sofia.

Chile and the Neoliberal Trap

The Post-Pinochet Era

ANDRÉS SOLIMANO

International Center for Globalization and
Development, Santiago, Chile

CAMBRIDGE UNIVERSITY PRESS
Cambridge, New York, Melbourne, Madrid, Cape Town,
Singapore, São Paulo, Delhi, Mexico City

Cambridge University Press
32 Avenue of the Americas, New York, NY 10013-2473, USA

www.cambridge.org
Information on this title: www.cambridge.org/9781107003545

First published 2012

Printed in the United States of America

A catalog record for this publication is available from the British Library.

Library of Congress Cataloging in Publication data
Solimano, Andrés.
Chile and the neoliberal trap : the post-Pinochet era / Andrés Solimano.
p. cm.
Includes bibliographical references and index.
ISBN 978-1-107-00354-5 (hardback)
1. Chile–Economic policy. 2. Free enterprise–Chile.
3. Neoliberalism–Chile. 4. Privatization–Chile. I. Title.
HC192.S618 2012
330.983–dc23 2012000797

ISBN 978-1-107-00354-5 Hardback

Contents

List of Figures   *page* ix

List of Tables   x

Preface   xiii

1. From Its Past and Present, Chile Is Poised to Provide a
   Better Future for Its People   1
   Introduction   1
   The OECD Route   2
   A Diverse and Rich Economic Geography   2
   Economic Progress: Contrasts, Contradictions, and
     Social Needs   4
   Features of the Post-Pinochet Democracy   10
   A Brief Tour of the Book   12

2. A Brief History: The Role of Authoritarian Conditions
   and Crises in Shaping Political and Economic Orders
   in Chile   16
   Introduction   16
   Enter Pinochet and His Repressive Military Regime –
     and the Free-Market Doctrine   22
   Chile's Post-Pinochet Democracy and the Administrations of the
     Concertación (center-left) Coalition   29
   Annex   34
   The Prevailing Political System of Chile has Emerged
     from a Volatile Constitutional Progression   34
   The 1833 Constitution Gave Preeminence to Strong
     Executive Power   35
   The More Liberal 1925 Constitution Extended Representative
     Government   35

Pinochet's Constitution of 1980   36
The Latest "Version" of the Constitution of 1980
    in the New Democracy Still Retains an
    Antipopular Flavor   37

3. Cementing Neoliberalism: A Cultural Revolution
    for the Free Market   39
    Introduction   39
    Free-Market Economics and Other Traditions   40
    The Complex Relation between Culture and
        the Economy   42
    From a Market Economy to a Market Society   43
    Cultural Contradictions   45
    Private Interests and Collective Action   46
    The Mass Media and the Narrowing of Public Debate   47
    Concluding Remarks   49

4. Economic Growth and Macroeconomic Performance in
    the 1990s and 2000s under Four *Concertación* Governments   50
    Introduction   50
    Burgeoning Economic Growth has also Come with
        Economic Downsides   51
    1940–1985 versus 1986–2009: Chile's Growth
        has Performed Much More Strongly in the
        Past Twenty-Five Years   51
    The 1986–1997 and 1998–2009 Periods: Economic
        Growth has Dropped off in the Twelve-Year-Period   57
    Chilean Growth in International Perspective   58
    Chilean Growth: Resource and Environmental Sustainability   58
        Can Natural-Resource Use Continue to be
            Sustained as an Export Base?   59
        Can Energy-Intensive Growth be Sustained?   60
        Can the Environment Continue to Withstand
            Rapid Growth?   60
    Chile as a Leader in Orthodox Macroeconomics   61
        Fiscal Policy: Running a Structural Surplus   63
        Exchange-Rate Policy: Still Grappling with Exchange-Rate
            Fluctuations   66
        Monetary Policy: The Overriding Objective of
            the Central Bank to Keep Inflation in Check   68
    Macroeconomic Policies and Performance under the *Concertación*
        Governments   69
    Concluding Remarks   72

5. The Social Record of the Post-Pinochet Administrations:
    Poverty Declines but High Inequality Persists   74
    Introduction   74
    Declining Poverty: Yes, but to What Extent?   76
    The (Qualified) Success of Poverty Reduction – Though
        Not Assured – Should Now Give Way to Targeting Income Inequality   78
    Growth, Poverty, and Inequality   82
    The Resilience of Inequality during Growth   82
    The Resilience of Inequality in a Democracy   84
    Conclusion: The Various Factors Explaining Persistent Inequality in Chile 85
    Annex: Taxation in Chile and in other OECD countries   89

6. The Social Policies of the 1990s and 2000s: Neoliberalism
    Tempered with Social Protection?   93
    Introduction   93
    The Social Policies of the 1990s   98
    The Social Policies of the 2000s   99
    Antipoverty Efforts   99
    Reforms in Education   100
    Health Sector   107
    Pension Reforms   110
    Labor Legislation and Unemployment Insurance   114
    Unemployment Insurance   115
    Levels of Unionization   116
    Concluding Remarks   118

7. Concentration of Economic Power: The New Elites of the
    Super-Rich, Oligopolistic Markets, and Dual Production
    Structures   120
    Introduction   120
    Wealth Concentration and the Chilean Super-Rich   122
    Market Concentration   124
    Concentration and Heterogeneity of the
        Production Structure   127
    Empirical Evidence of the Heterogeneity of the Chilean
        Production Structure: Micro, Small, Medium-Size, and Large
        Companies   129
    Concluding Remarks   134

8. Limits to Chilean Democracy and Governance
    for Capital   135
    Introduction   135
    Features of Chilean Democracy after the Pinochet Regime   137
    The Partially Reformed Constitution of 1980 Is Still Ruling   137

An Army-"Protected" Democracy (1990–2005)   138
The Binominal Electoral System   139
Nonelected Senators (1990–2005)   139
Democracy, Authoritarian Cycles, and Presidential Crises
   in Chile and Other Latin American Countries   140
Governance for Capital: Perceptions Indexes   144
The Business and Investment Climate   146
Concluding Remarks   147

9. Summary and Issues for the Future   149
Introduction   149
Economic and Developmental Institutions   150
Economic Growth   151
Democracy and Governance   151
New Social Contract: More Political and
   Economic Democracy   152

References   157
Index   163

Figures

4.1 Real GDP level and per capita index, 1985 = 100   *page* 52
4.2 Chile – Growth swings in 1974–2009   54
4.3 Chile – GDP growth has fallen from its historical marks
    in the 1986–1997 period   57
4.4 Chile – Evolution of the nominal exchange rates
    under two exchange rate systems, 1984–2010   66
4.5 Chile – The inflation rate under four
    concertación governments, 1990–2009   68
5.1 Chile – Income distribution – a steep slope down
    from the highest income groups   81
5.2 Chile – Growth and poverty have moved in the
    right direction but inequality remains high
    and flat, 1987–2009   83
6.1 Chile – Evolution of public, private, and private
    subsidized schools (panel A) and school enrollment
    (panel B), 1990–2009   102
6.2 Chile – Population distribution among health
    systems, 1990–2009 period (panel A), and distribution
    of population among health systems depending on
    income level, 2008 (panel B)   111
7.1 Chile – Market concentration in six sectors   127
7.2 Chile – Regional distribution of firms by size   133

Tables

4.1 Chilean economic growth and enabling factors:
A comparison between 1940–1985 and 1986–2009   *page* 53

4.2 Economic growth in Chile and emerging
economies, 1987–2009   59

4.3 Chile: Not enough progress is being made
toward clean energy, 2006–2010   60

4.4 Chile: Macroeconomic performance, 1945–2009   63

4.5 Chile: Main macroeconomic policies, 1990–2009   64

4.6 Gross and net central government debt   65

4.7 Chile: Volatility of the nominal exchange
rate, 1989–2010   67

4.8 Growth performance and macroeconomic
indicators across centrist-neoliberal policies
in the four administrations   70

5.1 Chile: Official poverty shows a drastic
decline, 1987–2009   77

5.2 Chile: Official and recalculated poverty for
2000, 2003, and 2006   78

5.3 Chile: Persistent inequality makes poverty
reductions a pyrrhic victory, 1987–2009   79

5.4 Gini coefficient: Selected countries, 2000–2008   80

6.1 Social matrix by government administration, 1990–2009   96

6.2 Labor union density in Chile and selected countries   117

7.1 Just four individuals (families) have an overwhelming
share of Chilean wealth   124

7.2 Chile: Employment, number of firms, and sales
by company size, 2006–2007   131

7.3 Sector and size distribution of the number
of formal companies, in percentages, 2003   132

7.4 Percentage share of exports by company
    size, 1999–2003   132
8.1 Evolution of political regimes in selected Latin
    American countries, 1960–2006   142
8.2 Presidential crises in Argentina, Bolivia, and Chile   143
8.3 Governance indicators for Chile, Latin American
    countries, and OECD, 2009   145
8.4 Business and investment climate: Argentina,
    Bolivia, and Chile   147

Preface

This book was written as an attempt to put some historical and analytical objectivity to the overly optimistic and uncritical assessments, so common over many years, of the Chilean economic and social model launched by the military regime of General Augusto Pinochet in the 1970s and 1980s, and continued and deepened – albeit with some modest amendments – by the various governments elected after the restoration of democracy in the 1990s and 2000s. The Chilean model was being enthusiastically promoted, at different points in times, by the International Financial institutions as the blueprint for stability, prosperity, and progress to be applicable in Latin America and emerging economies worldwide, while paying little attention to both the very particular economic and political circumstances under which it was implemented and its deleterious effects such as increased social inequality, large-scale natural resource exploitation, and the high concentration of economic power and political influence in a few elites. As of 2011, the Chilean establishment, the common citizen, and the international development community was shaken by the emergence of a strong, yet peaceful and creative, student and social movement critical of the profit motive and privatization of education in Chile, which began to demand fundamental changes in the economic model and more democracy for Chile. Interestingly, this social movement is led by a new generation of students and youth largely free of the experience, involving fond memories but also myths and ghosts, of the older generation that lived through the pre-military coup attempts of social reform and democratization and the subsequent collapse of democracy and military rule that affected Chilean society over the last half-century.

Comments by Alice Amsden, Jan Cademartori, Roberto Frenkel, and Manuel Riesco to a first draft of the book are greatly appreciated. I want to thank the important collaboration of my editor and friend Thomas G. Good who contributed fresh background research and enlightened editing and stylistic improvement to the overall shape of the book. Luis Valenzuela also provided important and unfailing support through very valuable and thorough research assistance, including index preparation, for which he deservedly has my thanks. Scott Parris, senior editor of economics and finance at Cambridge University Press, contributed with encouragement and empathy through the writing of this book. Adam Levine, Kristin Purdy, and Bindu Vinod were also supportive and effective in the coordination, editing, and production of this book. Finally I owe a debt of gratitude to my wife, Bernardita, daughters, Gracia and Paula, and son Pedro for their interest and patience over a period of three years while this book was being written.

1

From Its Past and Present, Chile Is Poised to Provide a Better Future for Its People

Introduction

In this introductory chapter, we provide a glimpse of Chile today – what it offers economically, socially, and in terms of democracy, as well as the challenges it faces in those dimensions. The focus of this book is on the political economy of the post-Pinochet transition in Chile, when the country tried to restore its democracy and keep the economy going along (largely) neoliberal lines, moderated by mildly improved levels of social protection and restricted by a constitutional charter oriented toward limiting political diversity, protecting the economic model, and ensuring the primacy of markets and the profit-motive over the state and social rights. The model yielded acceleration in the rate of economic growth that as of 2010 put Chile on top of the Latin American region, along with Argentina, in per capita income levels. The Chilean economic model launched in the mid-1970s pioneered, in a developing-country context, free-market and privatization policies, thus positioning Pinochet, along with Reagan and Thatcher, as one of the early political backers of free-market economics. Later, many Latin American countries, Central European countries, the former Soviet Union and the former Soviet bloc countries, and even China embarked on some variant of neoliberal economics, viewed as the solution to world economic and social challenges and the route to prosperity, progress, stability, and human welfare. The recent international financial crisis triggered in 2008–2009 and originated in the centers of world capitalism, such as the United States and some European countries; its aftermath – stagnation, debt problems, fiscal deficits, and unemployment – has started to shatter the dominance of market fundamentalism, both in economic theory and in public policy.

The OECD Route

In Santiago, Chile, on January 11, 2010, after twenty years of post-Pinochet transition, President Michelle Bachelet signed a membership agreement allowing Chile into the Organisation for Economic Co-operation and Development (OECD); Chile thus entered the club of thirty-one countries considered the elite economies in the world.[1] Of course, Chile's membership in the OECD is a testament to Chilean progress in the past twenty years, although for a developing country to be a member of a club of fundamentally rich countries has evoked some odd feelings.[2] As argued in this book, Chile has been on the move both economically and democratically. This does not imply, however, that in that same time span, the country has made the reforms necessary to include *all* its people under the umbrella of economic progress. In fact, despite the restoration of democracy with its limits and shortcomings in 1990 and the rise of per capita income (around US$14,000 in 2010), Chile is a country with inequality levels (of income, wealth, territorial development, access to social services, and so on) well above OECD standards and remains a case of economic development still distant from the prototype of the more mature, advanced countries that belong to the OECD. We believe, however, that the time is ripe for Chile to take the next step toward national "greatness" and further democratization if it can shed the harness of free-market dogma that serves well the economic interests of the elites but postpones opportunity for all.

A Diverse and Rich Economic Geography

Chile is that slender slice of land on South America's western edge that has an almost 3,000-mile coastline of the Pacific Ocean – a geographic

---

[1] Chile ratified the agreement on May 10, 2010. Twenty countries (eighteen European countries plus the United States and Canada) originally signed the Convention on the Organisation for Economic Co-operation and Development on December 14, 1960. As of 2011, thirty-four countries including Asian and Latin American countries have become members of the Organisation.

[2] Mexico and Turkey are two other developing countries that have chosen to enter the OECD.

advantage for trade. Bordered by Peru on the north, Bolivia and Argentina on the east, and Cape Horn on the southern tip of the South American continent, Chile is a country of diverse topological beauty. On its eastern border, Chile is separated from Argentina by the rugged Andes Mountains. Along the greater expanse of that range, Chile stretches through five major regions, each offering distinct ecological richness – and together offering a breadth of natural-resource exports and a burgeoning tourist industry.

Its arid Northern Tier (Norte Grande) contains the Atacama Desert, one of the driest deserts in the world, protected by the Andes from the prevailing winds and thus rainfall. It is here that Chile's large copper-mining industry is located, which along with other mineral deposits gives the desert its ochre hues. Just south is the Near North (Norte Chico), a semiarid region whose valleys provide broad ground for cattle raising and, more recently, fruit growing. Between the Andes and a range of coastal mountains (the Cordillera de la Costa) lies the belly of Chile – the Central Valley (Chile Central) – whose fertile land is home to Chile's agriculture, including its extensive wine vineyards, and most of its major cities, including its capital city, Santiago. The southern portion of Chile's Central Valley also contains depleted agricultural land that has been reforested for lumber, especially for the cellulose and paper industries. The southern tier of the country contains the South (Zona Sur) and the Far South (Zona Austral), which, moving southward, are home to pristine turquoise lakes formed from hundreds of rivers descending from the Andes (ideal for freshwater farming of various species of trout and salmon), rolling hills (ideal for raising cattle and producing milk, cheese, and butter), old-growth forests (augmenting its productive lumber industry), and then a continental coastline that features inlets, fjords, thousands of archipelago islands, and snow-tipped mountains. Both zones in the South attract a large number of tourists throughout the year, contributing to Chile's emergent service industry.

Santiago, the capital, located in the Central Valley, is home to approximately 40 percent of the country's population. In fact, according to the most recent census, 87 percent of Chile's citizens reside in urban areas, bunched largely in the Central Valley, southward from Santiago. The largest concentration of economic activity is in the Region Metropolitana, the greater Santiago area, another manifestation of the economic and administrative concentration of the country. Obviously, this urban congestion has its attendant problems, to which all urbanized areas are prey – pollution, overcrowding, crime, class segmentation (including large pockets of poverty), and other quality-of-life issues. Alongside the natural beauty of Santiago is the city's human geography – in which neighborhoods are stratified starkly by topography. The rich and the upper-middle class reside in the Barrio Alto (the higher parts of the city), and the working and lower-middle classes reside in the lower elevations of the city, where the factories are also located. This living arrangement is a microcosm of the pervasive inequalities that exist throughout the country.

Economic Progress: Contrasts, Contradictions, and Social Needs

Yet today, Chile is considered one of South America's most stable, (formally) democratic, and prosperous nations. It often ranks high in the major indexes used internationally to judge a country's performance, including economic freedom, perception of government corruption, global peace, global competitiveness, and prosperity. Among *all* countries worldwide, it usually scores in the top thirty in these same categories. In fact, according to the 2010 Index of Economic Freedom elaborated by the (conservative) Heritage Foundation, which measures liberalization in areas like trade, business, investment, the financial sector, monetary policy, property rights, the labor market, and the level of corruption (the Index is shy on labor rights and working conditions, however), Chile ranks 10th overall among 183 countries.

As mentioned before, in the Latin American and Caribbean region, Chile has one of the highest per capita GDP (in purchasing power parity), along with Argentina. Per capita GDP, however, overstates average living standards, as it is very unevenly distributed. It is here that dissimilarity with developed nations become apparent in the Chilean model. Its export base, albeit dynamic and vigorous, is heavily reliant on exhaustible natural resources; its private, for-profit pension fund system contributes to the development of capital markets, but a reduced number of pension fund management companies form the market and charge significant fees and offer limited coverage; and competition by the state or other agents is stifled by a powerful lobby.

Inequality is high by international standards and well above those of the OECD.

Chile also has an ample export base (although manufacturing exports are still not fully developed) and is highly committed to free trade, with an extensive and diverse trade network. It has the largest, most lucrative copper industry in the world whose benefits largely accrue to foreign corporations owing to a very liberal concessions system to exploit copper in Chile, ample agricultural products and seafood, a range of forestry and wood products, and a major niche in the international wine market. It has also entered into free-trade agreements with the European Union and a host of nations, including the United States, Japan, China, and Australia.

Nevertheless, its export composition does rely heavily on trade in commodities with volatile international prices. A concern is how long the Chilean export strategy can continue to rely so heavily on natural resources; for example, copper exports accounted for more than 50 percent of total exports in 2010, and primary products accounted for 68 percent of exports, with main industrial products consisting of processed food, cellulose, paper and wood, and chemical products. At some point, sustainability will become an issue, whether in the form of resource depletion or environmental/ecological consequences.

Chile is also ahead of the curve for extractive-industry countries that yield high returns for companies that enjoy low royalty and very favorable tax rates for nonrenewable natural resources. Low tax rates for foreign companies is a controversial policy given the relatively low share of copper-industry profits internalized by the Chilean state, particularly at times of record prices. Currently, no more than one-third of the copper industry is still state-owned (by the government conglomerate CODELCO, Corporación del Cobre down from approximately two-thirds by 1990 in a steady process of de-nationalization of the copper sector), and the capital-intensive and monopolistic nature of the industry means that it does not provide a substantial job-creating mechanism either within the industry or around it (in the form of value-added business support and supply services). Furthermore, like most extractive industries, its success depends on the worldwide price for copper, which fluctuates according to speculative mechanisms and changes in world demand.

In 2006, President Michelle Bachelet created an Economic and Socialization Fund to provide excess copper revenues for use during economic downturns – a fund not necessarily established by all countries where GDP relies heavily on extractive industries. As of December 2010, Chile has accumulated approximately US$13 billion in copper-driven reserve funding. In fact, in January 2009, President Bachelet earmarked more than US$1 billion of that fund to help middle-income families and smaller businesses endure the global financial crisis, US$500 million of which went to Chile's state-owned Banco Estado to provide credit for qualifying businesses and the other half to a fund that was to subsidize home purchases by middle-income families, thus creating more jobs in the construction industry. During the recession year of 2009, Chile spent nearly US$9 billion of the stabilization fund for countercyclical demand policies, and even so, GDP contracted by 1.7 percentage points in that year.

Chile also has in place a privatized pension system (AFP, Administradoras de Fondos de Pensiones) that is compulsory and against which the state cannot compete by offering pension fund management services. The AFP system is considered to have helped boost the country's capital market because it has encouraged domestic investment and savings. Nevertheless, the AFP charges high fees (compared with a public system) to contributors, a practice that ultimately diminishes pensions upon retirement. Similarly, Chile's private pension system has comparatively low coverage rates, reaching only those who are formally employed, which as of the first quarter of 2011 was only approximately 66 percent of the working population. Nevertheless, the reforms of 2008 extended universal minimum pension benefits, but they were funded by the state. Moreover, only six private AFP companies manage the retirement savings of millions of Chileans who neither have a voice nor participate in how those funds are used. Still, in spite of the pension reform of 2008, the state is prevented from running its own pension fund managing company, which could provide additional competition to the AFPs.

Since 1987, Chile's official poverty rate has fallen from 45.1 percent to 15.1 percent (in the United States, it ranges between 10 and 16 percent, varying annually); its "extreme poverty rate" fell from 17.4 percent to 3.7 percent. Some significant questions remain, however, about the true extent of the country's poverty reductions, as the official statistics are based on an outdated household-expenditure survey of the mid-1980s that measured consumption shares (even though there is a more updated version) and thus probably underestimates the poverty line, diminishing the share of the population below the poverty line. A study updating poverty lines (Larraín, 2008) for the 2000s using more recent consumption patterns shows poverty rates that are *twice as* high as the official poverty line. Chapter 5 analyzes this theme in more detail.

Moreover, Chile lags behind other countries on many environmental, technological, and social indicators. For instance, it is "vulnerable" on the SOPAC/UNEP Environmental Vulnerability Index; it does not place well on the Yale University/Columbia University Environmental Sustainability Index, and in both the World Economic Forum's Networked Readiness Index and the UN e-Government Readiness Index, Chile ranks outside the top thirty. The country spends less than 1 percent of GDP in research and development and, most woefully, is number 7 in Latin America and the Caribbean and number 48 (of 134 countries overall) in the World Economic Forum's Global Gender Gap Index (version 2010).[3] Particularly controversial has become the way it deals with the environmental impact of large investment projects such as Hydro-Aysen (a mega water-based energy generation project in Chilean Patagonia), which has given rise to popular criticism and rejection by environmental groups and the population at large. Chile's development strategy needs to enhance productive employment, environmental protection and restoration, and accessibility to information technology needs, and must unleash the market potential of Chile's small- and medium-sized businesses, which employ close to 80 percent of Chile's working-age population.

The Chilean development experience is rich and controversial. As hinted, each of these particular achievements also has its downside. But again, one cannot take away Chile's economic progress and its elevation to OECD status, although this move can create a sense of complacency and distract the country from its many pressing development

---

[3] The Networked Readiness Index is an international assessment of the impact of Internet Communications Technology (ICT) on the development process and the competitiveness of nations; and the e-Government Study Index measures the extent to which government provides accessible, valuable information on government policies, procedures, and processes on its Web sites.

needs. For these achievements, Chile can perhaps thank neoliberal, free-market economic policies – but with bitter irony. Since the mid-1970s, under the watchful eye of the U.S. government (in its broadest sense), free-market policies were first implemented as an experimental economic revolution under the military regime of General Augusto Pinochet, before Ronald Reagan and Margaret Thatcher popularized them as liberating economic imperatives. From the United States came the premier free-market economist Milton Friedman, who helped Chilean economists implement the neoliberal model under his attentive eye and with guidance from colleagues, mentors, and graduates of the University of Chicago's School of Economics. It was Professor Friedman himself who, in a self-congratulatory gesture, coined the phrase "the economic miracle of Chile."

Among the free-market-reform legacies implemented by Pinochet and his "Chicago Boys," which continued and exacerbated during the two decades of center-left governments, is excessive income inequality, which, at least since 1987, has persistently hovered between 53 and 56 percent, as measured by the Gini coefficient, a level that puts it among the top 10 percent in the world. This level is higher than most of its Latin American counterparts (except Brazil and a few others), higher than most countries and regions of the world (on par with four countries in sub-Saharan Africa), and much higher than what is typically considered by economic observers to be economically efficient. As a reference point, the OECD average Gini coefficient is close to 38 percent (the index ranges from 0 to 100, with lower numbers meaning lower inequality). In turn, as documented in Chapter 7, Chile has its own share of billionaires, who compete in the rankings of *Forbes* magazine with the super-rich of developed economies and emerging markets. Economic elites have become extremely rich and politically influential in Chile, and this process continues today.

In many respects, the Chilean social contract with its people – defined by its income inequality and many other social indicators – is disconcerting when it otherwise scores well along various economic dimensions. And it is counterintuitive in a country whose population has a "common cause" democratic experience in which both laborer and professional alike endured authoritarian regime rule from 1973 – the year of the military coup – to 1989, when the first democratic elections were held. Since then, four Concertación administrations have guided uneven economic progress under a version of the neoliberal model, complemented with more active social policies. But if Chile is to become a true "miracle" – to the extent that "economic miracles" exist – then it cannot continue to perpetuate an income gap and huge wealth disparities that could eventually polarize what is considered to be a cohesive society and that effectively thwarts building a middle-class and democratic society.

As the reader learns more about the economic and social landscape of Chile and its imminent challenges, some questions and issues will arise as threads that might be woven into a resolution.

Is Chile "tied to the hip" of Latin America in general, whose inequality is higher and percentage of middle class lower than in other nations and regions throughout the world? Or does Chile lag in and of itself because it is not yet unleashed from strict adherence to the neoliberal paradigm?

Why did the four social-democratic (Concertación) administrations that came after the Pinochet regime choose to maintain, on the whole, albeit with some variations, economic and social policies so close to the spirit of the Washington-consensus paradigm? Under the neoliberal paradigm that fostered rapid wealth accumulation largely for the rich, what types of jobs have been created? Did those administrations foster entrepreneurial activity at all levels? Did they integrate small businesses into economic progress? Exactly how did they respond to the income-inequality and middle-class dilemmas? For instance, one sign of an empowered middle class and a fairly treated working class is the existence of labor unions and civil society organizations that ideally should protect wage and compensation gains by laborers and workers.

Why has there been such a concentration of wealth during the last quarter-century or so in Chile? Who owns the wealth in Chile? Do the wealthy maintain their wealth because of an ineffective tax structure, monopolistic behavior, the nature of the global free market, or ineffectiveness or apathy by government? Why have they not created more jobs?

In Chile's free-market economy, does the fact that its copper industry and other mineral resources are largely owned by foreign companies that enjoy very favorable tax treatment contribute to income inequality, a concentration of wealth, and a phantom middle class, and if so, to what extent?

What should be made of the indexes in which Chile does not rate favorably: environmental vulnerability and sustainability, gender equality, unemployment, education and health, crime and violence, and social stratification?

In contrast, Chile has one of the highest ratios of military spending to GDP in the Latin American region: 3.5 percent (around US$6 billion), according to the Swedish International Peacekeeping Research Institute, SIPRI, which collects data on defense spending worldwide.[4] As a reference point, government spending in education was 4.4 percent of GDP in 2009. As of 2010, Chile was still devoting 10 percent of the gross revenues of CODELCO to the armed forces (this allocation is not scrutinized in parliament owing to a "confidential" law, the Ley Reservada del Cobre). This practice has certainly contributed to Chile's relatively high percentage of military spending. The center-right Piñera government has vowed to prepare legislation to phase out this law (in place for several decades) and replace the funding of the armed forces with a more transparent and accountable budgetary mechanism. The extent to which the armed forces, a powerful enclave in Chilean society, will receive fewer (or perhaps more?) resources after the eventual phasing out of the Ley Reservada remains to be seen.

Features of the Post-Pinochet Democracy

As we discuss in Chapters 2 and 7, Chile after the Pinochet regime is a case of an incomplete and "low-intensity" democracy. For nearly fifteen years after the departure of the military (between 1990 and 2005), nearly one-third of parliament was composed of nonelected, appointed senators; the president of the country could not remove the higher ranks of the armed forces; and the constitution ruling the

---

[4] Military spending in Argentina is 1% of GDP; in Brazil, 1.6%; in Bolivia, 2%; in Venezuela, 1.3%; and in the United States, 4.7% (see SIPRI 2011). According to the Chilean Budget Office (DIPRES), however, defense spending in 2009 was just 1.2% of GDP. For definitions of military spending and its international comparability, see http://www.sipri.org/research/armaments/milex/resultoutput/sources_methods/definitions.

country was approved in 1980 under a military regime and without electoral registers, free press, an operating parliament, and so on. In turn, electoral participation by youth is low, the ownership of mass media (newspapers and TV) is largely in the hands of big economic conglomerates of conservative bent, and the binomial system of representation penalizes small parties and the representation of independent movements in parliament. At the time of the writing of this book, after two decades of the restoration of democracy, Chileans abroad cannot vote for representatives in parliament or municipalities, or in presidential elections. Levels of labor union membership hover around 14 percent. In turn, independent and critical-minded think tanks and research centers are starving for funds and receive little help from an increasingly rich state.

In 2005, constitutional amendments eliminated "appointed" senators and senators "for life," reduced presidential terms from six to four years, and overhauled the criminal justice system to make it resemble the adversarial system of the United States. Given Chile's "amenability" to reconfiguring its constitutional foundation, how can the structure of Chile's highly centralized government be made more effective in order to capture the voice of Chile's more localized, territorial forms of regional government? It is too early to determine whether these modifications of the political system will manifest themselves as real changes for the people. Should Chile go further now rather than wait for the lagging effects?

Chile has a proud, vibrant, but perhaps counterintuitive history – a history of independence and a social fabric that has allowed the country to overcome authoritarianism and make enviable but uneven economic progress. This book, however, tries to dispel some myths of an exemplar democracy coming along with economic stability and progressive social policies does not always square well with the historical and contemporary record of the country. The political establishment (both center-left and center-right) has ensured a stable political equilibrium for two decades after the Pinochet regime. This balance, however, has largely excluded from parliament and other forms of political representation those who do not agree with the official consensus. The country must find a way to develop and empower its middle and working classes – to enable them to move into the same spheres as those who own (but do not rent) Chile's space – and it must thereby rectify its pervasive, persistent income and wealth inequality. Addressing the pending social agenda of lower inequality, rejuvenated public education and public health, broader social protection, and middle- and working-class participation effective national ownership of our natural resources such as copper, will require embarking on a new paradigm for economic growth and development, one that will require sharing opportunities for access to credit, capital, natural resources, and productive employment. A new social contract is needed for a fair economy and a more effective and participatory democracy.

A Brief Tour of the Book

This book is organized into nine chapters, including this introductory chapter. Chapter 2 analyzes the recent history of Chilean democracy and the economic model established in the mid-1970s, along with its variations afterward. The chapter shows that some critical institutions of Chilean democracy and its social contracts, such as the constitution, have historically emerged from either authoritarian junctures or interruptions of normal democratic practice. That was the case of the constitutions of 1833, 1925, and 1980, which are discussed. The chapter also highlights the various economic and political crises and reforms of the last forty years and shows that the dynamics of Chilean progress have been far from smooth and socially costless.

Chapter 3 demonstrates that the free-market economic model launched by the military regime in the mid-1970s was not only a program of macroeconomic austerity, market liberalization, and privatization, but also an attempt to introduce a new set of values and to change the culture of Chilean society around an idealization of the free market, the promotion of an individualistic ethic, and the legitimization of the profit motive extended to a vast array of new activities (education, health, pensions, roads use). The chapter highlights various areas in which a free-market cultural revolution unfolded such that it affected the cognitive day-to-day experience associated with the actual working of the market system, the teaching of economics in universities, the mass media, and the construction of a new common sense of the assumed virtues of the market in a country with weak regulation of the private sector and concentrated economic power in certain elites.

The chapter discusses Chile's path from a market economy to a "market society" (using the distinction of social scientist Karl Polanyi) and the adverse response to excessive marketization of Chilean society by social movements, as well as the cultural resistance by individuals to the widespread use of the profit motive.

Chapter 4 reviews the growth and macroeconomic performance of the Chilean economy in the last quarter century, placing it in the broader context of Chilean growth dynamics of the past six decades. The chapter documents the acceleration in GDP per capita growth since the mid-1980s, which has led to more than doubling the GDP per capita in the last twenty years but also identified a deceleration in growth rates since the late 1990s and throughout the 2000s. The chapter discusses the macroeconomic policy of Chile and its generally positive results but also notes Chile's adherence to the dominant orthodoxy of the 1990s and mostly in the 2000s, entailing independent central banks, inflation targeting, relaxation of capital controls, lack of intervention in the foreign exchange market (with some exceptions), and the attempt to conduct fiscal policy by predefined rules.

Chapter 5 analyzes the evolution of poverty and inequality and their relationship to economic growth and democracy during the past twenty-five years in Chile. The chapter documents the reduction in poverty along with the acceleration in growth but also presents evidence that actual poverty levels can be significantly higher than what is shown by the official statistics. Moreover, the chapter shows that inequality of income has been largely invariant regardless of economic growth (more rapid growth has not led to a decline in inequality) – a result that is at odds with the predictions of new political-economy theories that postulate an inverse relation between the two variables (growth and inequality). In addition, it explores a hypothesis about why the restoration of democracy and the election of four consecutive center-left governments did not spur policies that reduced inequality of income and wealth. The chapter discusses whether this corresponds to a change in the preferences in the electorate away from income redistribution or to a political system that tends to shield the economic elites from redistribution, with the post-Pinochet democratic governments lacking political will and capacity to break that blockade. Finally, the chapter summarizes the different factors behind the persistence of inequality as related to globalization, the wage structure, the educational system, the tax system, the power of capital, and the weakness of the labor unions.

Chapter 6 analyzes the evolution of social and labor policies in the 1990s and 2000s, connecting them with the social policies of the military regime and before. The chapter shows the attempts of the democratic administrations since the early 1990s to redress the main social gaps inherited from the authoritarian period and to start building a social protection network, but also the inability to put in place new, more progressive education, health, and pension systems that can break the structural tendencies of social differentiations that are the features of Chilean society. The chapter documents social reforms of the 2000s such as the Auge plan (health sector), the pension reform of 2008, the limited changes of the general law of education after a strong nationwide mobilization of secondary students, which challenged the prevailing for-profit education system and its large differences in resources and quality between public and private education (even though these changes did not really alter the segmentation and privatization of the education system, a central theme that emerged in full force in the student movement of 2011). The scope and limitations of these reforms are discussed in the context of the strong lobbies for private providers of social services, which try to protect their highly profitable niches in education, health, pensions, and other social activities in the face of weak attempts by the state to expand the reach of social protection and to democratize access to social services. As for the labor market, the chapter shows the continuity, in democracy, of policies oriented to maintain the flexibility of firing and hiring labor by enterprises and to keep the trade unions weak. The creation of an unemployment insurance scheme oriented toward workers in the formal private sector is examined, and its limits as a main device to protect people from the consequences of unemployment are highlighted.

Chapter 7 focuses on some main dimensions of the process of economic concentration of assets and market influence in Chile. It documents the emergence of a small class of super-rich that controls a substantial share of the productive national wealth and that compares well in terms of wealth levels to other super-rich worldwide. The chapter then discusses the degree of market concentration in finance, mining, pharmaceuticals, pension funds (AFP), health service, and insurance providers (ISAPRES), as measured by the

Hirschman-Hilferding Index. Then it analyzes the productive structure of the Chilean economy and its polarization between large enterprises and micro-, small- and medium-sized enterprises according to sales, employment generation, access to markets and technology, and export orientation.

Chapter 8 discusses several features of Chilean democracy from a regional perspective. It documents the alleged stability of Chilean democracy (interrupted by a military regime that ruled for seventeen years) by looking at the frequency of presidential crises in the past forty years in Chile and other countries in South America. The chapter also discusses some peculiar features of the post-Pinochet transition to democracy, including elements of a "guided democracy" that bestowed a privileged role on the military, the low level of civil society and popular participation in public policy making, the binomial system, and the prevalence of the authoritarian constitution of 1980. Finally, the chapter also documents progress in governance in dimensions such as rule of law, regulation, control of corruption, and quality of macroeconomic institutions as viewed by international (subjective) indexes based on perceptions of private investors and, to some extent, the general public. The chapter points out the contrasts between good governance for capital (property rights, macroeconomic stability, labor flexibility) and a limited economic governance for the majority of the population (weak protection of consumer rights, feeble regulation of big business, asymmetric information of companies and compliance with labor rights), as well as the limitations on overall democracy already highlighted.

Finally, a short Chapter 9 closes the book with reflections on Chile's recent experience with economic reform, development, and democracy and highlights areas of transformation and reform for more egalitarian, participatory, and democratic development in Chile in the future.

2

A Brief History

The Role of Authoritarian Conditions and Crises in Shaping Political and Economic Orders in Chile

Introduction

On September 18, 1810, *Criollo* leaders of Santiago (Spanish descendants born in the colony) declared independence from Spain; seven years later, on February 12, 1817, Bernardo O'Higgins Riquelme, the "father of Chile," defeated the Spanish and thereafter became supreme director of Chile. After Chile's first provisional constitution was approved by direct democratic vote in August 1818, conservatives and liberals engaged in a twelve-year turbulent period in which the country's constitution was changed four times according to whatever group attained power. But the fierce opposition of the conservatives, along with even stauncher resistance from the so-called *estanqueros* – politicians led by Diego Portales and associated with the *estanco* contract (regulating tobacco, liquor trade, and gambling) – led finally to their strident demand for a strong government and an end to social disorder.

After adopting a new constitution under conservative rule in 1833, Chile (according to official history) emerged as one of South America's most stable, politically advanced, and educated (by the standards of that time) nations, one about which the perception is that democratic government was largely the rule. As historian Gabriel Salazar (2009) points out, however, the critical foundational moments of the modern Chilean state – the approval of new constitutions in 1833, 1925, and 1980 (see the Annex to this chapter) – were actively influenced by the Chilean military; they were not necessarily the result of democratic decision making with popular participation. Consequently, the constitutions that formed the basis of the subsequent social contracts emerged from ad-hoc constitutional commissions appointed by the executive power and not by the deliberations of elected constitutional conventions, in a process often surrounded by different degrees of latent or open violence and by influence of the military.[1]

From 1833 into the 1880s, Chile embarked on its process of nation building, strengthening its republic. But by 1889, the seeds of civil war were brewing, with growing and open hostility between the president of the country, José Manuel Balmaceda, and the government's congressional leaders. In 1891, President Balmaceda allegedly overstepped legal boundaries by issuing an official budget that Congress deemed beyond the mandate of the office, and a majority of congressional members signed an Act of Deposition against the president. The two sides eventually squared off when congressional leaders began to form an organized resistance with the support of the navy. With the army remaining faithful to the executive, the two sides (the president versus the parliament, and the army versus the navy) engaged in a bloody seven-month civil war in which, after the death of some 10,000 combatants, the "revolutionaries" emerged as victors over President Balmaceda, who committed suicide rather than submit to trial. And although the 1833 constitution remained in place, congressional leaders chose to interpret it in their favor, establishing a stylized "parliamentary" system in which the national parliament indirectly controlled the reins of government by enacting "periodical laws" (*leyes periódicas*) that took power away from the executive branch by controlling presidential nominations, the appointment of cabinet members, and perhaps most important, the budget. The president remained the head of state but with largely weakened powers.

The semi-parliamentary system that emerged after the civil war of 1891 remained in place until 1924, when Arturo Alessandri Palma[2], the dissident liberal president who had been elected in 1920, was ousted in a military coup by the "September junta." Just four months later, however, the September junta was ousted in another military coup by the "January junta," to forestall what they believed was a massive conservative power shift in the country. After the coup d'etat, Alessandri

[1] See Benitez and Rosas (2009).
[2] The father of Jorge Alessandri Rodriguez was president between 1958 and 1964.

returned to power, promising the masses that he would begin implementing social reforms. He stayed in power long enough (resigning
nine months into his term) to authorize the new constitution of 1925,
which ceded greater powers back to the president's office. The constitution of 1925 was preceded by attempts at popular participation
in its formulation. In fact, a Constitutional Assembly of Workers and
Intellectuals (*la constituyente chica*) with 1,250 delegates from the different provinces, social organizations, and political parties representing
working- and middle-class people gathered and opened discussions for
shaping a new constitution to be followed by a broader Constitutional
Assembly. After hesitation and doubts, President Alessandri, under
pressure from the military, ruled out calling a Constitutional Assembly,
appointed a small commission to draft the new constitution, and called
for a plebiscite to ratify it.[3] The new constitution established a balance
between the executive, the parliament, and the judiciary, overcoming the semi-parliamentarian system and creating the basis for more
modern social legislation and broadening of social rights. With some
amendments, the constitution of 1925 survived until September 1973.

Foreshadowing the U.S. presence and influence in Chilean political
and economic affairs that supported Pinochet's power grab in 1973, government officials decided to create the Office of Comptroller General
of the Republic (Oficina de la Contraloría General de la República)
under the influence of an American adviser, Edwin Walter Kemmerer,
the noted Princeton economist who was called the "money doctor"
for his consultancy to various governments to promote strong curren-
cies and balanced budgets. In Chile, he was influential in establishing
the Central Bank of Chile, creating a Superintendence of Banks and
putting Chile on the gold standard. These reforms helped attract massive foreign investment from the United States as well as loans to the
government.

This initial period of the new constitution, however, was marked
by divisive intragovernmental and interparty disputes and conten-
tiousness during what came to be the start of Chile's "presidential
republic," in which four different presidents, including Alessandri
again, headed the government until 1938. From 1938 to 1952, the
Radical Party (built on the same principles of liberty and equality that

---

[3] See Grez (2009).

gave birth to the French Revolution) held power, and it embarked on an import-substitution industrialization policy that created a sector for such state-owned enterprises as copper, steel, and energy and established a mass education program, a national health system, and a pay-as-you-go social security system. Helped by a renewed social contract that reached out to various elements of the population, and particularly the middle and working classes, Chile maintained a relatively participatory and stable democracy during the period. Social movements in Chile had historically been organized by the working class, which had been concentrated originally in natural-resource activities but now also extended to the industrial and service sectors, dominated by government enterprises and other government agencies.

The last of the Radical Party candidates was Gabriel González Videla, who served as president from 1946 to 1952, in what could be considered an interlude of partial democracy in which Chile was to suffer from an array of political, social, and economic instability. President González was eventually to turn his back on the principles of his own party – for example, proscribing the Chilean Communist Party (under pressure from the United States, which proved to be one mark against him), curtailing labor rights and repressing strikes, and taking a tough stance against social movements and protest demonstrations. He proved, in fact, to alienate almost all groups – his own party (not to mention the opposition), parliament, and the people themselves.

González Videla in his anticommunist zeal prosecuted Senator Pablo Neruda, his former head of propaganda in the presidential campaign, who went into hiding and then exile to Argentina. Neruda later on, in 1971, was granted the Nobel Prize in Literature for his contribution to world poetry.

After González Videla left office, democracy returned to the masses from the early 1950s into the 1960s, with an electorate that participated vigorously and knowledgeably in elections. Significantly, a "new" political party emerged as electorally important during the period – the Christian Democrats, a group of largely disaffected conservatives and social Christians who wished to move Chile toward more centrist policies and promote social reforms. The most important of the candidates from this party was Eduardo Frei Montalva, who was elected president in 1964 and embarked on a cautious program of agrarian reform, economic stabilization, the "Chileanization" of U.S.-owned copper interests, and more inclusive credit policies, as well as a progressive social agenda that included the emergence of a loose social alliance of urban dwellers (*pobladores*), peasants (*campesinos*), students, and labor unions, besides clear policies to expand educational opportunities to the poor. Although economic growth from 1960 to 1969 averaged a respectable 4.9 percent annually (with average per capita GDP growth at 2.5 percent), annual inflation remained stubborn at around 25 percent, and the country lived with chronic balance-of-payment deficits and fiscal imbalances.[4] Moreover, as the second half of the 1960s began to unfold, the social movements seen early in the Frei Montalva government, augmented by the winds of social unrest blowing across the rest of Latin America (the Cuban revolution was influential at that time) and the world in general, were calling for greater democratization and popular participation in government policy. In Chile, it was the start of more significant labor unrest, fuelled by the current capitalist mode of economic organization: the unwanted presence of foreign-owned enterprises in the country, a fatigued import-substitution policy that discouraged exports and was thus inimical to growth, chronic inflation, and persistent inequality. All these began to drive Chile toward the left-leaning (pro-working-class) elements of presidential politics. At the same time, the accelerated pace of democratization, popular participation, and economic redistribution was being resisted by the upper-income groups within Chilean society, creating social tension.

In 1970, Salvador Allende, a candidate of Unidad Popular (UP) – an alliance of socialists, communists, and disaffected Christian Democrats grouped into two parties, Movimiento de Acción Popular Unitaria (MAPU) and Izquierda Cristiana, or the Christian Left – rode a left-wing surge to win the election but with only 36.3 percent of the popular vote. President Allende quickly began implementing policies around a program called the "Chilean way to socialism," in which a transition to Chilean-style socialism (different from that of the Soviet Union and Cuba) would be accomplished through legal and constitutional means. In an effort to break up the concentration

---

[4] Ffrench-Davis (1973) provides a complete reference of economic policies in the 1950–70 period. Meller (1997) contains a long-term overview of the Chilean economy. Bitar (1979), Larraín and Meller (1990), and Maldonado (1993) provide analyses of the Allende experience.

of economic power in the capitalist class, large industrial holdings and banks were brought into the hands of the state, in the so-called *area social*; and, according to the electoral platform of Allende, those holdings would be composed of no more than ninety large enterprises considered to have wielded monopolistic power in industry and to have provided the material base of the dominant economic elites. The foreign-owned copper mines were nationalized by law with unanimous vote (among the Left and Right) in parliament, and agrarian reform was accelerated. Politically, President Allende himself (who was a former government minister, a senator for many years, and who served as president of the Senate in the 1960s) sought a "neo-socialist" agenda in which economic reform in support of the working class would coexist with policies seeking to transform and deepen a representative democracy that was considered elitist and devoid of popular participation but still respected. Despite intense disagreement between the moderate and radical elements of the Unidad Popular coalition over political strategy and elements of the economic program, the UP's official platform did not call for central planning or the dictatorship of the proletariat.

President Allende pursued an expansionary fiscal policy and an increase in wages to stimulate aggregate demand and called for a price freeze (also imposed half-heartedly in 1971 by U.S. President Richard Nixon) and land reform. As mentioned before, the UP government went on to de-privatize or nationalize the country's U.S.-owned copper mines (as well as its coal and steel); the majority of private banks; and beyond the original plan, almost 500 private companies (including most of the country's textile firms and U.S.-owned IT&T). After a rapid increase in growth and employment in 1971, the result of the first set of policies was a fiscal deficit (financed by money creation), a zooming inflation rate, product hoarding, a burgeoning black market, and instability in both the countryside (as peasants began seizing land held by wealthy landowners) and urban areas (as workers tried seizing some small and medium-sized firms that were not included in the official program of nationalization). The result of the second set of policies was perhaps more dire. Nationalization angered the United States, which effectively embargoed trade with Chile (and by most accounts began a covert policy to undermine Chilean reform and political processes, with the blessing of Secretary of State Henry Kissinger and President Nixon); it also drew the ire of the World Bank, which between 1971 and 1973 severely cuts loans to Chile to almost zero.[5]

The result was a flight of foreign capital, a cut in foreign aid, withdrawals of money from banks, financially stressed industries, hyperinflation, the exhaustion of international reserves, and a fiscal deficit of nearly 25 percent of GDP – in effect, a sabotaged economy and an increasingly divided nation, with strikes by labor, a disaffected middle class that was taking the brunt of the economic hardships, and a capitalist class that was afraid Allende was laying the groundwork for a socialist country that would expropriate its economic and political power.

In fact, evidence suggests that Allende tried placating those who were being alienated from the center of politics – including the wealthy capitalists and the military. One of his appointments was Augusto Pinochet, whom Allende named commander-in-chief of the Chilean army in August 1973 because Pinochet, a disciplined soldier, conscientiously followed the president's orders when other military personnel, most of whom were middle class, were expressing their dissatisfaction with the left-wing government. Both the supreme court and the parliament, however, had denounced what they believed was Allende's usurpation of government power, and Pinochet adroitly surmised where true power resides. Although Allende still believed in Pinochet's loyalty when first learning of rebellion by the armed forces on the day of the military coup, Pinochet saw that he was just one step away from controlling Chile.

Enter Pinochet and His Repressive Military Regime – and the Free-Market Doctrine

On September 11, 1973, Pinochet and a four-man junta seized control of the government, ousting Allende, who died in the assault on the presidential palace, the Palace of La Moneda.

Pinochet's brutal repression of Allende supporters, workers, students, and intellectuals in the weeks immediately following the coup, a practice maintained for years during his regime, is well documented by both sides. By most accounts, the number of citizens that his secret

[5] Bowen (2006).

police, the National Intelligence Directorate (DINA), created in 1974, detained, imprisoned, tortured, or executed (including those who "disappeared") almost certainly extends beyond the figures cited by the Rettig Commission.[6]

Box 2.1 General Augusto Pinochet – His Role in the Republic in a Nutshell, so to Speak

General Augusto Pinochet Ugarte was appointed commander in chief of the Chilean army on August 23, 1973, by President Salvador Allende. Nineteen days later, Pinochet headed the military coup that ousted President Allende and its government; bombed the presidential palace; declared martial law and a state of siege; closed parliament, radio stations, and newspapers; and arrested and deported thousands of Allende supporters, many of whom were summarily executed by the military. Originally, the military junta was to have had a rotating presidency among the commanders in chief of the four military branches (army, air force, navy, and the national police). Pinochet, however, soon consolidated his control of the junta, first retaining sole chairmanship and then proclaiming himself "supreme chief of the nation" (the de facto provisional president) on June 27, 1974. He officially changed his title to "president" on December 17, 1974. Under the 1980 constitution, Pinochet remained president until October 1988, when, despite his repression of political opposition during most of his regime, he was compelled by social pressure and also by some elements of the armed forces to fulfill his constitutional obligation to hold a national referendum, which rejected his serving an additional eight-year term.

After a transitional period between the plebiscite of 1988 and the accession of an elected government in which the junta and the new

---

[6] The Rettig Commission was a nontrial "truth" tribunal established by the first democratically elected president after Pinochet's reign, Patricio Aylwin, to investigate human rights violations under the regime – specifically, "disappearances after arrest, executions, and torture leading to death committed by government agents or people in their service, as well as kidnappings and attempts on the life of persons carried out by private citizens for political reasons" (cited in Hayner, 2001). Some believe, however, that the number of persons cited as "disappeared" in the report (approximately three thousand) is overinflated (BBC News report, December 30, 2008, www.bbc.co.uk), and the report remains controversial for all sides. Other accounts consider that this number underestimates the actual number of deaths and "disappearances."

coalitions negotiated a free election, Patricio Aylwin, supported by a center-left coalition consisting primarily of Christian Democrats and socialists, took office as newly elected president of Chile on March 11, 1990.

After the restoration of democracy in 1990, Pinochet remained the commander in chief of the army until March 1998, a critical peculiarity of the Chilean transition to democracy. Then, after stepping down as commander in chief, he became a senator-for-life – a privilege granted by the 1980 constitution to former presidents with at least six years in office (the last two constitutionally elected presidents, Frei Montalva and Salvador Allende, had already died). His status as senator meant he was immune from legal prosecution in Chile.

The start of the real downfall of Pinochet was a private visit in 1998 to the United Kingdom, where he met, for tea, with former prime minister Margaret Thatcher. In that visit, Pinochet was arrested following an extradition request issued by Spanish judge Baltasar Garzón. Pinochet was apprehended by Interpol and held in London under house arrest from October 1998 until March 3, 2000, when he was returned to Chile after protracted pressure from the Chilean government of President Frei Ruiz-Tagle, who pressed a diplomatic and political offensive for the return of the general on grounds that he would be investigated and prosecuted in his home country. In Chile, he was subject to a variety of judicial proceedings for corruption, tax evasion, and elimination of opponents, and was occasionally placed under house arrest, but he was never indicted or convicted by the Chilean judicial system. In 2004, however, a U.S. Senate committee investigation of money laundering headed by Senators Carl Levin (D-MI) and Norm Coleman (R-MN) uncovered a network of more than 125 bank accounts at Riggs Bank and other U.S. financial institutions apparently used by Pinochet and his close associates for covered money dealings. Pinochet died in the tranquility of his house in Santiago on December 10, 2006.

The military regime, after an initial flirtation with nationalistic economic policies, heralded a new economic era for Chile – and became an experimental dawn for neoliberal, free-market economics. To help the Pinochet regime implement these policies, approximately twenty-five economics experts, Chilean-born but trained at the University of Chicago School of Economics in the United States (and thus termed the "Chicago boys"), were recruited into important decision-making positions by the military junta. Their agenda called for abolishing price controls, deregulating markets, reducing import tariffs in an effort to boost exports and cheapen imports, bringing down the inflation rate by establishing macroeconomic discipline (through a drastic fiscal adjustment program in 1975 in which nearly 100,000 public employees were separated from the state sector in one year), restoring property to its former owners, and securing external credits.[7] As mentioned in Chapter 1, Professor Milton Friedman, the famed Chicago School economist (later earning a Nobel Prize in Economics), backed these reforms philosophically and personally by lecturing in Chile, advocating that a free market would bring a free society.[8] Later on, in 1981, another Nobel laureate, Professor Friedrich von Hayek (famous for *The Road to Serfdom*, written in the early 1940s), visited Chile and gave support to the ongoing free-market revolution carried out by a repressive military regime.

Chile soon became the fastest-growing economy in South America. By 1978, inflation had been cut to approximately 30 percent and lowered even further later on with a combination of shock treatment in aggregate demand and exchange-rate-based stabilization. Trade liberalization, privatization, fiscal adjustment, and market-liberalization policies dominated the policy agenda of the second half of the 1970s. In the two years up to mid-1981, there was a real appreciation of the exchange rate against a fixed parity of $39 per U.S. dollar and ample inflows of foreign capital. Investment and consumption boomed, and banks were lending heavily both to other banks and to economic conglomerates still in fragile shape. In the late 1970s, the economy, at last, started to show some positive figures: GDP grew an average of 8.1 percent per year in the 1977–81 period (per capita it grew 6.5 percent). Exports grew 16 percent on average in that period, faster than ever before, and reached historic levels in 1980, matched only seven years

---

[7] Ironically, despite movement away from state intervention – one of the three pillars of the neoliberal economic-growth paradigm – Pinochet did not return the copper industry and other important mineral resources to foreign ownership and, in fact, put them under state control. The state company, Codelco, was founded in 1976.

[8] A book by Kornbluh (2004) unveils compelling, previously classified audio and textual evidence of U.S. involvement in efforts to overthrow Allende and prop up Pinochet, with CIA, Kissinger, and Nixon involvement.

later. Furthermore, the fiscal budget ran consecutive surpluses in the period, after at least fifteen years of deficits, and the central bank built international reserves as well, peaking in 1980 at US$4 trillion. Inflation was cut down from 340 percent in 1975 (174 percent in 1976, 63.5 percent in 1977) to 9.5 percent in 1981.

Although the exchange-rate-based stabilization program between 1978 and 1982 reduced inflation, other economic indicators such as employment and solvency of the financial sector were hurt by accumulated overvaluation of the Chilean peso, which led to a loss of economic competitiveness and distorted patterns of credit allocation. As early as 1981, the economy was entering a severe economic and financial crisis.[9] The current account deficit had climbed to a record 14 percent of GDP, and the risk profile of banks' loan portfolios increased in the face of insufficient banking regulation by the authorities. The combined effect of a reduction of an unsustainable deficit in the current account of the balance of payments, adverse terms of trade and external interest rate shocks,[10] the cut-off on domestic credit by a largely bankrupt banking system, and the reduction of real wages following the depreciation of the peso all led to a sharp decline in demand for private consumption and investment during 1982. The cut in aggregate demand and plunging investment brought about a rapid decline in output and income, primarily in 1982 but bottoming out in late 1983. Between the peak level of the third quarter of 1981 and the bottom level of the same quarter of 1983, per capita income was at 75 percent of its level in the late 1960s, and the cumulative decline in GDP in the two years was -16 percent. Inflation had itself almost more than doubled from its low level of 9.5 percent in the twelve months prior to December 1981.

A crisis in the banking sector quickly developed, with recurrent currency devaluations and serious external debt servicing problems. And many small and medium-scale firms drowned in debt or went

---

[9] References for that period are Ffrench-Davis (2002), Edwards and Edwards (1987), Solimano (1993, 1999), Foxley (1983), Corbo and Solimano (1991), Meller (1997), and Solimano and Pollack (2007).

[10] The recession in Chile coincided with the 1982–3 recession in Latin America, which was forced by the sharp rise in interest rates in the United States, declining terms of trade, and a sharp cutoff of foreign loans. It was followed by what is known as the "lost decade," the fourth-largest economic downturn after the Great Depression.

bankrupt, with an ensuing destruction of organizational capital and jobs. With the decline in real wages and an escalation in the cost of living, the share of absolute poverty increased. In turn, the open unemployment rate skyrocketed to around 20 percent of the labor force by 1982. Moreover, free markets under Pinochet again came at a dear human price, and they made other countries in the area and those who governed them resistant to market reforms, as they equated economic liberalization with political authoritarianism.

The economic crisis and depression triggered immediate pressures on the government to change its policies. The government's initial reaction as early as 1981 was to reiterate its commitment to free-market policies and thus to refrain from intervening – a course that had to be abandoned when the severity of the crisis soon became quite clear. The government decided to abandon the fixed exchange rate policy of thirty-nine pesos per dollar in June 1982, which had been followed for three years. This decision implied a devaluation of the Chilean peso; in the next three months, it depreciated from thirty-nine to sixty-three Chilean pesos per U.S. dollar. This policy was supposed to benefit exporters and import-competing sectors, but it also sharply increased the foreign debt-servicing burden (in local currency) and deteriorated the balance sheets of firms that had borrowed in dollars (but whose revenues were in pesos in commitment to the fixed exchange rate), probably believing that the fixed exchange rate system implemented by the government would last forever. To control the unfolding financial crisis, the government instituted, first, a large debt-relief program based on a preferential exchange rate for debtors in dollars; and second, a takeover of the management of several banks in distress with a large stock of nonperforming loans (see Box 2.2). These relief programs were financed with the issue of treasury and central-bank bonds to be placed with domestic investors, particularly the new private-pension funds emerging from the privatization of the social security system in 1981. These policies were supported with loans from the IMF, World Bank, and IDB. The social consequences were dire.[11]

---

[11] Solimano, Aninat, and Birdsall (2000) discuss the array of social consequences ensuing from the policies to deal with the crisis of the early 1980s.

Box 2.2 Experimental Neoliberal Policies Created Fast Growth but Forced the Government to Intervene in the Banking Sector in the 1982–1983 Crisis

Between 1981 and 1986, the government interceded in the operations of twenty-one financial institutions, either liquidating or rehabilitating them. Later, those banks were privatized. Almost all these interventions, which included banks and financial institutions, occurred between 1981 and 1983. Small banks and financial institutions were liquidated, and some banks were soon sold to foreign investors. For the two large Chilean banks first slated for government intervention in November 1981 (Banco de Santiago and Banco de Chile), a resolution was facilitated by the acquisition of portion of their assets and liabilities by foreign banks, with small branches operating in the country. The interventions in seven banks and one finance company in January 1983 were different from those of 1981 and 1982. The government's intention was to accelerate the resolution of the ongoing crisis by sending a signal that both the owners and the creditors of distressed institutions would have to incur some of the losses and reduce the rollover of loans that pushed interest rates to very high levels.

In the case of the three institutions that the government liquidated in 1983, domestic creditors suffered a loss equal to 30 percent of their claims (foreign depositors were compensated in full by the government). The fiscal cost of the financial crisis of 1982–3 amounted to close to 40 percent of GDP.

By March 1986, Banco de Chile and Banco Santiago needed to be recapitalized. Their reprivatization was part of the *capitalismo popular* (popular capitalism) scheme in which new shares were sold to small investors among the general population. The government's intention was not to maximize revenue but rather to expand the number of new shareholders so as to "deconcentrate" ownership, given that the concentration of ownership in the conglomerates, or *grupos económicos*, had been an important reason for the crisis. As a result of the sale of the two newly viable banks, 88 percent of Banco de Chile's total capital and about 95 percent of Banco Santiago's was raised from the new shareholders. The new owners, or *capitalistas populares*, owned preferred stock and were entitled to receive dividends of up to 30 percent of bank profits.

The mix of economic gains and social distress brought about by the Pinochet government's policies came along with a repressive style of government. Direct military rule started in 1973 and was then extended by nondemocratic plebiscite in 1978; in 1980, another plebiscite (also with dubious transparency and competitiveness) approved a new constitution that gave Pinochet sweeping executive power until 1990. Needless to say, this constitution was not prepared by a Constitutional Assembly but by an ad hoc commission and the state council, which in 1980 presented a constitutional text to the military junta (see Annex). The junta, after some revisions, gave thirty days for calling a plebiscite for popular ratification of the new constitution.[12]

In 1988, however, partly in response to social mobilizations in previous years, to long overdue international pressure, and to Pinochet's certainty that he was untouchable, the general opted for another plebiscite to extend his rule even further, for another eight years. But the emergence of a broad coalition of leftists and centrists – which had led to massive public protests and relied on broad-based information dissemination to reach a large portion of the voting public, thus compelling a record 92 percent of the population to register to vote – delivered a commanding "no" vote against Pinochet and swept into power a coalition that came to be known as the Concertación.

Chile's Post-Pinochet Democracy and the Administrations of the *Concertación* (center-left) Coalition

On December 14, 1989, the people of Chile engaged in their first free and open election in nearly twenty years, electing the majority of new members of a two-chamber Parliament, as well as a new president, Christian Democrat Patricio Aylwin, the candidate of the Concertación, who received 55 percent of the vote. President Aylwin served from 1990 to 1994 in what would be considered a transitional

---

[12] As we mentioned in the Annex, the constitution also created the National Security Council, whose role is to advise the president on matters related to national security. The National Security Council is presided over by the president of the republic and consists of the presidents of the Senate and of the supreme court, the commanders in chief of the armed forces, and the general director of the armed police. Moreover, ministers of the interior, foreign relations, national defense, and finance can also participate in the council but without the right to vote. Since the constitutional reforms of 2005, it can be convened only by the president of the republic.

phase, although the notion that Chile, in the first decade of the twenty-first century, is still in "a transition to democracy" continues to linger in the current political debate. The Concertación was able to forge a consensus among groups with different views and interests. As part of talks between the Pinochet government and opposition about the transition from the military regime to a democratic government, it was able to assume power[13] by agreeing to support the fundamentals of the neoliberal economic model in place and to refrain from actively seeking judicial prosecution of whoever was ultimately responsible for the massive violations of human rights that took place during the military regime (remember that Pinochet was to remain commander in chief of the army). An uneven social partnership between (strong) capital and (weakened) labor was encouraged within a policy framework favorable to private investment, along with a cooperative, deferential attitude from what remained of organized labor, which had survived the active repression and legal changes oriented to reduce the power of the labor union movement in the 1973–89 period. In the context of a fragile recovering democracy, labor demands (including further unionization, higher wages, and more extensive labor rights) were not encouraged. The implicit notion was that private investment would reign supreme over the economy, a feature that was to be accentuated in the next twenty years of post-Pinochet transition, although the state started to invest more heavily in social sectors and infrastructure, two areas largely neglected during the military regime.

The Aylwin administration, conscious of the accumulated social demands and fragile social conditions of the poor and working class, raised taxes at the outset to fund social programs in an attempt to reverse the social deterioration inherited from the military period while also raising the minimum wage, increasing monetary subsidies to the poor, and providing more money to chronically underfunded public health and educational systems. Fiscal resources were also

[13] In 1986, an affiliated armed branch of the Chilean Communist Party, the Frente Patriótico Manuel Rodrigue (FPMR), attempted a massive importation of arms and weapons from abroad that arrived in a north coastal region of Chile called Carrizal Bajo. The purpose was to train and arm a parallel army to overthrow the regime. This ultimately failed, as the regular army seized the shipping and confiscated the weapons. As a last straw in this strategy, the FPMR undertook on September 8, 1986, a failed assassination attempt by gunfire of General Pinochet in an ambush that took place in the Cajon del Maipo, a mountain valley at the base of the Andes near Santiago.

devoted to revamping public infrastructure – ports, roads, and high-ways – which had deteriorated after years of public-investment neglect. Macroeconomic policies in the 1990s were targeted at accommodating higher social spending while also reducing inflation, in addition to tax-ing short-term capital inflows and reducing public external debt.

In the next election, December 1993, Christian Democrat Eduardo Frei Ruiz-Tagle, the son of former president Frei Montalva, who pre-ceded Allende, led the Concertación coalition to victory with a clear majority of votes, at 58 percent.[14] During his administration, President Frei Ruiz-Tagle somewhat "retilted" Chile toward the neoliberal par-adigm, by privatizing the water sector, closing down coal mines, and overseeing the modernization of the Chilean economy by integrating it more fully into the international community. He signed free-trade treaties with Canada, Mexico, and various Central American countries, and during his tenure Chile became a member of MERCOSUR, the World Trade Organization, and the Asia-Pacific Economic Cooperation (APEC) group. Still, Frei kept an eye also on the social landscape. During Pinochet's regime, Frei had been instrumental in establishing the Free Elections Committee, and he campaigned actively for the "no" vote on the 1988 plebiscite to return to democratically elected govern-ments. In running for presidential office, Frei pledged to alleviate pov-erty and to put more women into public office – indeed, he appointed three women to his cabinet. In addition, Frei was more generous in his minimum-wage policy and tried to undertake countercyclical fiscal policies to protect employment and cope with the aftermath of the Asian crisis in Chile in the 1998–9 years.

In 2000, socialist candidate Ricardo Lagos was elected president, but contrary to his nominal party affiliation and perhaps to show that a post-Allende socialist could take power and avert hints (or ghosts) of returning socialism and eventual anti-neoliberalism, President Lagos

[14] The Frei Montalva administration was responsible for initiating many reforms in Chilean society, including *promoción popular* (social promotion), *reforma agraria* (agrarian reform), *reforma educacional* (education reform), and *juntas de vecinos* (neighborhood associations) among the main projects. Frei Montalva later became an active part of the opposition against Pinochet's military government. But in 1982, Frei Montalva died in Santiago, reportedly from a postoperative infection from stomach surgery. His death, however, has been a matter of controversy, with credible allega-tions that he was actually poisoned by the Pinochet regime. The former president's family filed a lawsuit, which was still pending as of 2010.

actively courted representatives of big business and high finance, dampened the potential activism of organized labor, and postponed changes in labor legislation. He also moderated environmental demands from ecological groups, and although he presented legislation to remove several provisos of the constitution of 1980, he fell short of calling for a referendum to undertake comprehensive reform and to rewrite the constitution approved under Pinochet. A critical democratic reform that had been pushed even by President Frei Montalva in 1980 and other leaders of the opposition to Pinochet in the 1980s, such as the election of a Constitutional Assembly to draft a new constitution for Chile, was not in the cards for the Lagos administration. A Constitutional Assembly would draft a new constitution and then ratify it by popular vote to replace, with due popular legitimacy, the 1980 constitution. On the economic front, the socialist presidents of the 2000s (Lagos and Bachelet) were quite orthodox in economic matters. Lagos, a Socialist, did not depart from (broadly) neoliberal policies, although he did introduce a public health reform to extend health coverage for several chronic illnesses to working- and middle-class people, the Plan Auge (see Chapter 6). In turn, he devoted important efforts to upgrade and modernize the physical infrastructure with strong private-sector participation through user-fee schemes. The macroeconomic policies of the Lagos government were fairly orthodox. His economic team furthered conservative fiscal policies by adopting an explicit rule to run a structural fiscal surplus (see Chapter 4), achieved a further reduction in inflation but suspended the tax on short-term capital inflows, and supported a floating-exchange-rate regime with minimal central-bank intervention.

In March 2006, the Socialist Party candidate, Michelle Bachelet, assumed the presidency as the fourth administration from the Concertación. Ms. Bachelet, a charismatic and charming lady, single mother, non-Catholic, who was put in jail in the 1970s and then exiled for activities of resistance to the Pinochet regime, was the first woman president in the history of Chile. She initially tried to rule under the banner of a "citizen's government" and "parity government," meaning, respectively, independence from the dictates of the ruling political parties that formed the coalition supporting her government and equal representation of men and women in cabinet appointments. These two purposes, independence from political parties and gender equality at the ministerial level, were relaxed later in her administration. On the economic front, she appointed a neoliberal finance minister with strong academic credentials (a professor at the Kennedy School of Government at Harvard) and strongly empowered him – with regard to the rest of the cabinet and the political parties backing her government – with the double aim of keeping public finances in order (or in surplus) and to resist pressures to change in a progressive direction, the prevailing economic model, whether coming from disaffected sectors of the Concertacion, the labor and student movements, environmental groups, or pro-redistribution constituencies. Her main social reform was of the social security system, extending universal pensions payments and rights to all eligible citizens. As discussed in Chapter 6, these reforms left almost untouched the profitable private pension system of the AFP. In the first three years of Bachelet's tenure, Chile enjoyed a spectacular surge in copper prices, which generated current account surpluses in the balance of payments and a large fiscal surplus on the order of 7–8 percent of GDP. Average economic growth in 2006–7, however, did not accelerate much (GDP growth was 4.6 percent), creating the strange combination of a sharp terms-of-trade boom and relatively modest growth.[15] Later on, Chile was hit by the effects of the financial crash of 2008 in the United States and Europe, leading to a contraction in economic activity of 1.7 percent in 2009 and an increase in unemployment of close to one million workers. Nevertheless, Chile avoided a banking crisis, and the financial crash in the advanced economies worked their impact mainly through trade, capital inflows, and the real side of the economy. The savings made by the Bachelet government and placed in assumedly safe financial assets in the United States during the bonanza years allowed the government to implement countercyclical fiscal policies without having to borrow abroad.

In retrospect, it is apparent that the four democratic Concertación administrations that ruled between March 1990 and March 2010 tried

---

[15] This anomaly may be explained, in part, by a fiscal policy oriented toward saving most of the terms-of-trade bonanza on deposit abroad (primarily in U.S. banks) as part of Chile's Economic and Social Stabilization fund, established by President Bachelet in 2006 (more on this fund in Chapter 4). In fact, by end of 2008, Chile held more than US$20 billion in the surplus fund – this in addition to nearly US$23 billion in international reserves held by the central bank.

to strike a certain balance between continuing the neoliberal economic paradigm and addressing the most evident social effects of
free-market policies – focusing primarily on poverty reduction and
increased social protection for the most vulnerable groups initially
(the extremely poor, the elderly, and women and children) but later
also for the "middle class," making available about US$1 billion for
home loans from the Stabilization Fund. Concertación policies, however, never really tried to address the complex issue of the persistent,
long-term disparities in income and wealth distribution; in turn, the
center-left coalition allowed a big concentration of wealth in the hands
of powerful and politically influential economic elites. As we show in
this book, these inequalities are among the highest not only in Latin
America but throughout the world. The mantra of these democratic
administrations, "growth with equity," has been satisfied more regarding the first half – namely, economic growth (and still not fully). But
equity must wait for a definitive policy paradigm unless we identify
equity as equivalent to reducing poverty (a work also still far from
complete), which, in any case, has largely been a by-product of Chile's
growth acceleration. Unfortunately, prosperity will not be shared with
broader segments of society until a social contract in which "opportunity" and "access" become part of a truly socially oriented market
economy is drawn up.

Annex

The Prevailing Political System of Chile has Emerged from a Volatile Constitutional Progression

Since its first strides toward independence, Chile has had ten constitutions. The first three (1811, 1812, and 1814) were attempts to legitimize
its independence from Spain. After the expulsion of the *realistas* (the
group that supported the Spanish monarchy) and during the O'Higgins
government, two more constitutions were written, in 1818 and in 1822,
both with a marked nationalist spirit. Another in 1823 was written by
conservative Juan Egaña but was largely a discordant initiative at a
time of mounting liberalism.

After a failed attempt in 1826 to establish a federal regime in Chile,
a new constitution was written in 1828 by Jose Joaquín Mora, a Spanish

liberal. But by 1831, the conservatives and the *estanqueros* had seized power, and in the spring of that year a "grand constituent convention" was summoned to subdue the populist, anti-aristocratic, anticlerical dialect of the 1828 constitution.

The 1833 Constitution Gave Preeminence to Strong Executive Power

The new constitution that emerged by May 1833 was oriented toward a strong presidency. The president of the country was allowed two consecutive five-year terms, and the office held extensive power over the cabinet, judiciary, public administration, and armed forces. The 1833 constitution was markedly centralist, with political hegemony residing in the capital city of Santiago, a feature that still defines Chile's highly centralized administrative and political system today.

The More Liberal 1925 Constitution Extended Representative Government

In 1924, social discontent with the elitist politics of the conservative government and the continued negation of broad social rights for almost 100 years prompted young officers from the army to demand political change in a movement called "*ruido de sables*" (that is, they literally "rattled their sabres in their scabbards" in protest). Their demands for political reform led to the writing of a new constitution.

The 1925 constitution stated the official separation of church and state, which was the culmination of the gradually eroding political and economic power of the Roman Catholic Church. It provided legal recognition of workers' right to organize themselves into labor unions, promoted the social welfare of all citizens, enabled the state to restrict private property for the public good, and increased the powers of the president in relation to the bicameral parliament in place after the defeat of the liberal administration of President José Manuel Balmaceda in the Chilean civil war of 1891.

The new constitution extended presidential terms from five to six years but did not allow consecutive terms. It established a system of proportional representation for parties with slates of candidates up for parliament. The government was divided into four branches, in descending order of power: the president, the legislature, the judiciary, and the comptroller general (authorized to judge the constitutionality of all public sector actions, the correct use of public property, and transparency in financial management of the fiscal budget).

Pinochet's Constitution of 1980

The constitution of 1925 fell prey to the military coup that overthrew the Allende government on September 11, 1973. A new constitution was drafted by the Ortuzar Commission, appointed after the 1973 coup; it was then modified by the *junta de gobierno* (military junta) between 1978 and 1980. On the seventh anniversary of Pinochet's military takeover, the government issued a controlled plebiscite in which the new constitution was "approved" by Chilean voters in the absence of electoral registers, free press, and other constitutional guarantees. The constitution is still in place today, with several modifications.

The 1980 constitution legally sanctioned the immense powers that had already been adopted by General Pinochet and promoted three major tenets of neoliberalism – the supreme value of private property, severe restrictions on the state in its economic role as producer (with the exception of its copper industry, the main provider of funding for the military), and a severe clampdown on labor rights. The constitution called for an eight-year transition period, in which the military government – with Pinochet as the reigning president, and his National Security Council, formed by the heads of the navy, air force, and national police (which comprised the military junta), as the reigning legislative branch – would give way to a civilian government. The constitution originated the notion of a "protected democracy" by making the armed forces the "guarantors of the institutional order." During that eight-year period, the junta, via the National Security Council, would be allowed to enact "temporary provisos" to maintain an "orderly" transition, and it was immune from any standard democratic controls or oversight. A clause was included that prevented any civilian president from removing the commander in chief of the army, navy, and air force without the consent of the National Security Council (this proviso was nullified after the constitutional reforms of 2005, whereby a civilian president can effect removal but only after congressional approval). In addition, the upper house of parliament, the Senate, was to include eleven nonelected members (see Chapter 8).

The Latest "Version" of the Constitution of 1980 in the New Democracy Still Retains an Antipopular Flavor

When the New Democracy reassumed control of the presidency in 1990, after Pinochet was defeated in the 1988 plebiscite, it introduced Chile's current "binominal" electoral system. In 1988, the opposition to the regime negotiated with the military junta to enact Law 18,799 – the Constitutional Organic Law on Popular Elections and Vote Counting. Since 1990, the two main political coalitions in Chile, the center-left Concertación por la Democracia (Concertación for short) and the center-right Coalición por el Cambio (formerly the Alianza por Chile in the 2000s), have shared political power in Chile in parliament and later in the executive. The system has brought "stability" but also has restricted political representation of positions that do not fall within the agenda of (restricted) democracy and free-market economics, which have dominated the political spectrum after the demise of the military regime.

Consequently, during the twenty years following the military regime, legislation passed in parliament had to be negotiated only with the center-right political party and not with representatives from the (non-Concertación) left or other independent social and political forces outside of the two main coalitions, as they simply were not present in parliament. No doubt, the political and economic legislation that has passed since the restoration of democracy in 1990 has tilted toward more conservative positions.

In 2005, more than fifty constitutional reforms were approved by parliament but not ratified by popular referendum. They were intended to eliminate some of the remaining, more undemocratic areas of the text – for example, the nonelected senators (appointed senators and senators-for-life) and the prohibitions against the president's removing the commander in chief of the armed forces. They would also have reduced the president's term of office from six to four years and the powers of the National Security Council. In an ironic turn, however, the reforms of 2005 allowed deputies and senators to assume positions in governments (say, as state ministers), a feature ruled out in the electoral system existing before the coup of 1973. This allowed political parties to appoint their replacements in parliament without having to go to popular vote. Thus, the practice of appointed senators was not eliminated after all.

These reforms led President Lagos to make the controversial declaration that Chile's transition to democracy was complete. A more accurate definition of "transition completion" could have included a democratically elected Constitutional Assembly that would draft a new constitution to be sanctioned, in turn, by popular vote. In contrast, no new constitution has been voted on after the restoration of democracy in Chile in 1990.

3

Cementing Neoliberalism

A Cultural Revolution for the Free Market

Introduction

The free-market model launched by the military regime in the mid-1970s was not only an economic program of market liberalization and integration with the global economy. It was also an attempt to introduce a new set of values and to change the culture of Chilean society. It amounted to a cultural revolution. This new utopia was built around an idealization of the free market, the promotion of an individualistic ethic, the legitimization of the profit motive extended to a vast array of new activities (education, health, pensions, roads use). The new view also held a hostile (or at least reluctant) attitude toward the traditional roles of the state as a producer, regulator, and redistributing agent.

Cultural revolutions to support emerging economic or political revolutions are not new in history. In the 1960s, the Chinese leader Mao Tse-tung launched a cultural revolution to subvert what he considered remaining individualistic values and counterrevolutionary tendencies in party leaders and state officials and to remove remaining "capitalist attitudes" in the population. Mao's Cultural Revolution was oriented toward both consolidating his own personal power and creating the value and cultural base supportive of a highly egalitarian, communist, and communal society.

In the new Chilean economic order, led by the unrelenting pursuit of profits, there was little room for active labor unions, social movements, and state protection of social rights. A new cultural hegemony was needed.

We can highlight four areas in which a free-market cultural revolution unfolded: the cognitive day-to-day experience associated with the actual working of the market system, the teaching of economics in universities, the construction of a new "common sense" around the virtues of the market by public intellectuals and the media, and the narrowing of political and social debate in Chilean society. Let us discuss some of them.

Free-Market Economics and Other Traditions

Today the teaching of economics in Chilean universities (as well as in many universities around the world) is dominated by neoclassical economic theory complemented by neoliberal economics[1] (a radical version of free-market economics viewed not only as a theory but also as an economic and political project to be imposed on society).[2] Young generations have been trained (indoctrinated?) in the narrative and analytics (helped by cozy math and graphs) of the virtues of free markets and individualism. This theory – known as utilitarianism or rational choice – is based on a rather narrow vision of the motivations of human behavior. Neoclassic theory views individuals as truly calculating machines that maximize utility ("happiness"), a direct function of consumption. This theory implicitly assumes that individuals are endowed with great capacities to process costs and benefits of different choices available to them. There is increasing consensus, however, that this is a highly reductionist approach to human nature. People in the real world have a wider set of motivations besides selfishness, including altruism, solidarity, generosity, and group-oriented behavior. In fact, human beings are not the cool processors of costs and benefits depicted in the neoclassic theory but real people seeking rewarding social interactions within and outside the family, including engagement in collective actions and social movements when conditions are ripe for them. Moreover, passions and irrationality cannot be ruled out in people's behavior.[3]

---

[1] See Kaletsky (2010) and Harvey (2010).
[2] The financial crisis of 2008–10 is leading to a questioning of this paradigm. Neoclassic theory originated in the works of Jevons, Bentham and Mill, Alfred Marshall, and Wilfredo Pareto, who assumed that people act in an individualist manner looking to achieve their maximum level of utility and satisfaction.
[3] For further critical discussions of these motivations, see Marglin (2008), Quiggin (2010), Sen (2009), and Jackson (2009).

In Chile, like in other nations, the spell the "invisible hand," developed by the Scottish philosopher and economist Adam Smith – in which the pursuit by each person of his or her individual interest (profit or utility) would be compatible with the harmonious well-being of society as a whole and with overall market efficiency – has certainly been influential in the legitimization of the free market. How to square this hypothetical construct with the daily evidence that markets and working conditions in real-world capitalism are plagued by the effects of asymmetric information, routine abuse of the consumer, nonprice considerations, alienation in the workplace, advertising-induced overconsumption, monopolistic practices, and so on is an open question.[4]

The promotion of an idealized free-market vision by the media, the universities in their training of students, and the discourse of public intellectuals and commentators has led to the emergence of a new common sense apparently dominant in Chilean society, albeit criticism of the (neoliberal) common sense is appearing around the questioning of the profit motive and the charge of high fees in universities, among other issues. In fact, the ideology of the free market collides with the cultural tradition of Chile, strongly influenced by the teachings of the Catholic Church[5] and other religious denominations as well by civil-society organizations, schools, and political parties that historically have encouraged social behavior oriented toward collective projects of different natures, such as social solidarity, charity, delivery of social services, community organization, and progressive social transformation.

---

[4] As is well known, Adam Smith was a professor of moral philosophy at Glasgow University in the eighteenth century who wrote about ethical and moral topics and their influence on human behavior. See A. Smith (1759 [2007]). It is apparent that Adam Smith's real vision was more nuanced and complex than suggested by his later popularity (somewhat similar to what happened, from another perspective, with Karl Marx).

[5] The topic of the moral basis of capitalism has always been present in the social thought of the Catholic Church and is reflected more recently in the writings of popes John Paul II and Benedict XVI. Even Pope Benedict XVI has cited the concept of alienation in Marx. The Vatican has been traditionally suspicious of the moral consequences of capitalism (and communism) because of the disruptive effects on values and the family inherent in economic systems based on the search for profit, individualism, and self-realization through material consumption.

The Complex Relation between Culture and the Economy

Economics and the social sciences have formulated different theories about the origin of values and culture and their causal relationship to the economic system. Max Weber (1905 [2001]) highlighted the importance of religion, especially the Protestant ethic, which rewards savings, work, and the accumulation of wealth, in facilitating the development and spread of capitalism. In effect, the transition from a feudal and traditionalist system to capitalism needed a value structure that accommodated capital accumulation and technological change and accelerated a social mobility quite different from the feudal order, which was based on the divine origin of authority and tradition. In Max Weber, it is clear that causality goes from values (affected by religious preferences) to the economic system. This is not the only line of causation or mutual interaction, however, between values and culture and the material basis of society. Karl Marx (1848 [1979]), in his effort to contest the Hegelian idealistic philosophy that prevailed in the early to mid-19th century, stressed the role of the economic structure, modes of production, and concomitant social relations in shaping ideas, beliefs, values, and ideology in society.[6] Marx postulated, therefore, a line of causality (albeit his analysis did not mention this term) different from that of Max Weber. In his study of capitalism, Marx highlighted the "commoditization" of human work under conditions of wage labor and the creation of a market for labor power in which the typical worker has little or no control of the production process – which differed from the craft of the skilled artisan worker under previous, precapitalist economic formations. Karl Marx also emphasized the alienation of workers in the capitalist factory system.[7]

Although Marx maintained a dialectical view of historical change and considered capitalism a system that permanently revolutionized modes of production, the alleged "economic determinism" associated (probably wrongly) with his name was contested by the social thinker and leader of the Italian Communist Party in the 1920s, Antonio Gramsci, who developed the concept of "cultural hegemony."[8] This

---

[6] For a philosophically oriented treatment of the issue, see Wolff (2003). An economist's perspective is provided in Foley (2006).

[7] See Hobsbawm (2011).

[8] See Forgacs (1988).

concept refers to the prevalence within and acceptance by the general population of the beliefs, values, and ideas of the dominant social classes. These become "common sense" and therefore appear as shared by vast groups. In turn, this common sense helps to maintain the legitimacy of the economic and social system. In Gramsci, ideas and culture could be even more important than traditional forms of political power based on coercion for the maintenance and cementing of social orders.

It is interesting to note that since the days of the military regime, one can observe in Chile a type of "economic determinism" in policy making, reflected in the absolute priority given to the maintenance and consolidation of the economic model – seen as the definite pathway to development, welfare, and self-realization for Chileans – over the existence of democracy under the military regime and the deepening of democracy (one more participatory and less elitist) during the center-left governments after the military regime. A concrete manifestation of the priority given to economic management is the overriding power given to finance ministers by different governments (the military regime and the Concertación governments) from the mid-1970s until today (the Piñera government could perhaps be an exception to this).

From a Market Economy to a Market Society

There exists a tradition in economics and the social sciences (rarely taught in economics courses) that emphasizes the risks for social cohesion and community values of a society excessively based on the logic of the market. In effect, authors such as Karl Polanyi and Daniel Bell cautioned against the perils of extending the logic of the market to all human activities in the pursuit of a market society rather than a market economy.[9]

Polanyi in his book *The Great Transformation* (1944) postulated his idea of a "double movement": on one side the extension, many times led by the state, of the logic of the market and profit to areas that were not being reached before the advent of capitalism (he emphasized the labor market and the market for land and natural resources

[9] See Polanyi (1944), Bell (1976).

as "fictitious" markets). A second (counter) movement consists of reaction and resistance to the extension of the market to new realms previously dominated by public goods and community provision. This resistance can take place at the individual level or through collective action carried out by the student movements, labor unions, environmental groups, civil society organizations, and religious groups. Historical examples of this countermovement were the promotion of labor and social-protection laws (a minimum wage, prohibition of child labor, pensions, regulated workweeks, etc.) and, more generally, the creation of the welfare state.

In Chile, the first movement to impose a market economy (more precisely, a market society) in the 1970s was blunt. It was associated with the Pinochet regime and entailed suppressive policies toward social and labor movements, the banning of political parties, and the curtailment of free press and other civil liberties. This was not motivated only by the need for Pinochet to consolidate his regime politically but also to facilitate the consolidation of the market society. The extension of the reach of the market in the last three decades in Chile has included spheres such as private schools, the private provision of health services through the ISAPRES system, the private system of pensions (AFP; see Chapter 6), not to mention the encouragement of consumption (along the lines of a consumer society, with the United States as the implicit model). This led to an expansion of retail trade, shopping malls and suburban neighborhoods, and a culture of debt and consumption. To support the increase of consumption, in a growing economy with modest wages due to inequality in income distribution, we witness the pervasive expansion of consumer debt provided by banks and unregulated retail companies and other lenders, all supported by a burgeoning industry of advertising intended to create new wants and desires in the population.

The entry of the market in the provision of social services (examined in more detail in Chapter 6) generated a high degree of social differentiation and exclusion in the access to good quality education and other social services according to the capacity of users to pay. Acceptance of the new system was not easy, and waves of conformism have coexisted with social protest. The use of (expensive) student loans by university students to finance fees and tuition and the debts incurred by the middle class for durable goods, housing, travel, and other amenities are a main source of anxiety in working families. More generally, we can posit that waves or cycles of social response to free markets and nonparticipatory politics in Chile has taken place at different points in time during the past three decades: one was in the 1983–7 protests against the economic crisis and authoritarian politics of the military; then in 2006, with the eruption of a secondary student movement critical of the privatized education system; and again in 2011, with the student and environmental movements for the recovery of public education and against the profit motive as applied to the universities and schools.[10]

Cultural Contradictions

Daniel Bell in his classic book *The Cultural Contradictions of Capitalism* argued that, while capitalism was able to bring an unprecedented level of material progress and leisure opportunities, the system also encouraged high consumption levels, thereby weakening the drive for savings, thrift, capital accumulation, and delayed gratification, features required for productive capitalism to strive and flourish. In addition, Bell also stressed that capitalism in its drive for expansion and "marketization" of all activities alters and dislocates social relations, shattering the requirements of stability, predictability, and security that people want at personal and familial levels. According to Bell, these are the main cultural contradictions that any capitalist society has to deal with.

Both Polanyi and Bell emphasized that the structure of values, social norms, and culture in society is very important for moderating the negative impact of the free market and unbridled capitalism on social cohesion, the family, the community, and the environment.[11]

---

[10] The newly democratic governments that followed the military regime were also apparently afraid of the social movement and labor unions that reemerged in the 1980s and contributed decisively to the social and political dynamics that eventually led to the departure of the authoritarian regime. The center-left governments encouraged a sort of consensus politics with the center-right political parties rather than seeking alliances with labor unions, student movements, and a plethora of other civil society organizations empowered by the end of the authoritarian regime. A practice of social demobilization, conformism, and elitist politics ensued.

[11] Culture and ideology are important supportive and reinforcing elements of any social order, as emphasized by Marx and Gramsci, among others.

Private Interests and Collective Action

To understand the processes of social dynamics relevant to grasp the Chilean experience of the past three decades, it is useful to refer to the work of social scientist Albert Hirschman. In the late 1970s, the author wrote a small book entitled *Shifting Involvements: Private Interest and Public Action*, which attempted to explain why people, in certain periods of their lives and the history of their countries, chose to dedicate themselves to activities of public policy and collective action, whereas in other periods they lent themselves to private activities, oriented to the market and the accumulation of wealth in conformity with the status quo.[12] In Hirschman (1982), people go through cycles alternating between public (collective) involvement and private pursuits. These cycles seem to fit, broadly, into the global historical experience of social movements and individual action of the past few decades.[13] The dominant motivations of the collective-action phase are the common good (as subjectively understood by the individual) and the undertaking of collective projects, according to Hirschman.[14] This behavior clearly has a component that goes beyond material interest and utilitarian logic and seeks transcendence through idealism, solidarity,

---

[12] The argument Hirschman uses is a variation of a topic that comes from Aristotle, picked up by the philosopher Hannah Arendt in her book *The Human Condition*. In that book, the author elaborates on the distinction between "active life" and "contemplative life." The active life could be the dedication to public matters or to commerce and industry. The contemplative life, which Greeks gave a higher value, was dedicated to the cultivation of science, art, and knowledge.

[13] The 1960s and 1970s witnessed big waves of collective action: the "French May," the "Italian hot autumn," the "Prague spring," the Mexican student activism (and its later repression) previous to the Olympics games, and others. In addition, we find the pacifist movement in the United States against the Vietnam War in the 1960s and the drive for social reform and social change in Latin America and other countries. These movements may be characterized by a greater influence, compared with other decades, before or after, of collective action around certain utopian ideas and social projects. A "market motivation," with the pursuit of self-realization through private activities and material well-being, may describe better the motivations dominant in the decade of the 1990s and 2000s in several countries associated with the eruption of free-market economics and neoliberalism. Naturally, in any historical period, both types of motivations (collective action and individualism) mix and overlap.

[14] In the earlier reasoning given for changes to individual activity dedicated to the private and public area lies the postulate that the structure of values and preferences can change over time. This is in contrast to the utilitarian theory, which supposes stability and exogeneity of these preferences.

social responsibility, and contribution to the community and the fate of other people.[15]

In this context, political apathy, conformism, and lack of citizen participation in public matters, such as those observed during most of the post-Pinochet transition in Chile, may be due, according to Hirschman, to a disappointment with collective ideals that may be considered failures. The violent end of the project of the Unidad Popular in 1973 was, besides the human tragedy this entailed, a great disappointment to many people who afterward turned to private endeavors. Of course, not all individuals choose the road of private endeavors and resignation rather than political activity in periods of setbacks. Apparent political apathy and conformism may also be due to the lack of a supportive environment (weakening of public universities, lack of state funding for independent think tanks) for critical thinking and social organization associated with a constrained transition to democracy.

The Mass Media and the Narrowing of Public Debate

The mass media play an important role in shaping cultural hegemonies. The evolution of the Chilean press during the military regime is well known. Right after the military coup, in September 1973, all newspapers that supported Allende were banned, and a strict censorship of the press (TV, newspapers, magazines) was put in place by delegates of the military junta. The main newspaper that was allowed to circulate during the whole military period without interruption was the conservative *El Mercurio*, a publication that consistently supported the military regime throughout its different phases. The newspaper *La Tercera* was also authorized to circulate right after the military coup. The situation became somewhat more relaxed in the 1980s, when alternative and independent newspapers and magazines were allowed to operate.

Contrary to expectations, however, the restoration of democracy did not lead to substantive diversity of views and critical thinking in the media. In fact, in 1990 a main blow to the existence of

---

[15] Another motivation for public action may be more mundane and lies in the search for power, with the prestige and privileges that holding power positions entails. In contrast, private-oriented motivation in relation to production, accumulation of wealth, and consumption is emphasized by the utilitarian theory and neoclassic economics.

independent and critical mass media that started to flourish in the later years of the Pinochet regime took place. It is reported that the Aylwin government made an active effort to limit and discourage the financial support coming from abroad for the array of independent publications that had developed in the 1980s, such as *Revista APSI, Análisis, Fortín Mapocho*, and other media critical of the military regime. Probably it was envisioned that these media could also be a source of critical scrutiny of the new democratic government. The curtailment of financial support for the independent media proved deadly for the survival of these publications, as foreign-based support was not replaced by state advertisements.[16] In contrast, most of the state advertisements during the center-left governments went to *El Mercurio* and *La Tercera*.[17] The pro-Concertación newspaper *La Epoca* also disappeared for lack of economic support. Thus, twenty years after the restoration of democracy, more than 90 percent of the newspapers in Chile are controlled and owned by two national conglomerates – *El Mercurio* and *La Tercera* – both of conservative bent. In turn, open-air television channels are dominated by a strict market logic in which viewer ratings and revenues from commercials represent the bulk of their income and guide, without balance, the content of TV programs and newscasts. As mentioned in Chapter 1, the Chilean state owns a TV channel (Television Nacional de Chile), but this channel does not receive direct budgetary allocations from public coffers and is forced to follow the strict market logic of self-financing by selling commercial time. Recently, a major TV station owned by the Catholic University of Chile and the church was privatized and acquired by a big conglomerate (the Lucksic group, who was the top-ranking Chilean member of the *Forbes* list of billionaires in 2010). In turn, another TV channel previously owned by the largest public university, Universidad de Chile, was privatized in the 1990s. At the time of the writing of this book, that TV station was sold again to Time Warner, an American telecommunications multinational corporation.

---

[16] In the political context of the new democracy, apparently subscriptions by the public were not enough to keep these media alive.

[17] See Mönckeberg (2009).

Concluding Remarks

The economic transformation into a free-market economy is not only a technocratic exercise of aligning relative prices, exchange rates, budgets, taxes, and so on but also a cultural and ideological transformation to enable a society to accept working according to the profit motive and dominant private property. This chapter explored the role in the legitimization of the free market of various "cultural" mechanisms such as universities teaching neoclassical-neoliberal economics and the messages transmitted by the mass media and public intellectuals toward building a new "common sense" necessary for an unrelenting capitalist economy. The extension of the market to social sectors and other fields reveals the attempt to build a market society, in the terminology of Karl Polanyi, in Chile. The movements to introduce this market society by the military and its further consolidation and attempted legitimization in democracy is documented. The chapter also highlighted the cultural and social response and resistance of the student movement and civil society, labor unions, and grassroots organizations to the profit motive and the retreat of the state in education and other fields that has been recently observed in Chilean society, as well as the difficulties in enforcing a market society in unequal countries.

4

Economic Growth and Macroeconomic Performance in the 1990s and 2000s under Four *Concertación* Governments

Introduction

Although free-market, neoliberal reform began in the 1970s under Pinochet, economic growth in fact achieved a harvest more steadily in the second half of the 1980s and more fully in the 1990s – that is, ten to fifteen years after the policies of macroeconomic stabilization, external opening, privatization, and liberalization of financial markets were initially launched. At the same time, economic growth has slowed since then: the average growth rate in the first decade of the twenty-first century is 3.7 percent per year, nearly half the growth rate of 7.3 percent from 1986 to 1998, the "golden years" of economic growth. By the 1990s, the restoration of democracy had given a degree of domestic and international legitimacy to the Chilean economic model, particularly in financial circles and mainstream public opinion; in turn, the belief was that rapid growth had helped legitimize an incomplete democracy, and it introduced a climate of social and political stability as democratic political leaders continued to pursue the economic model inherited from the Pinochet regime with some variations. The slowdown in growth, however, along with mounting inequality may now be a signal that the New Democracy must be deepened and extended so as to retain its apparent legitimacy and the social tranquility it initially engendered. Maintaining reasonably rapid economic growth has been the cornerstone of the economic strategy of the past two decades of the post-Pinochet administrations. Nevertheless, as current events in Chile as of the writing of this book show, aggregate economic growth by itself has ceased to be a sufficient condition for giving legitimacy to an economic model perceived as rendering unequal results.

In fact, it is clear that an emphasis on economic growth – and the macroeconomic policies to make it possible – has been at the expense of insufficient attention to broader social issues affecting all Chilean people (see Chapters 5 and 6). Moreover, it has come on the back of a surging export base, which may have dire environmental impacts on the horizon.

In this chapter, we examine what has driven Chilean economic growth and macroeconomic performance – whether it has been the (tempered) neoliberal policies of the four Concertación administrations, the prevailing external environment under their tenures (that is, the result of the broader process of globalization), or a combination of both. This analysis of both macroeconomic performance and economic growth sets the stage for an analysis of the broader social agenda, discussed in the next chapter, so that as a newly installed member of the OECD, Chile can reduce its level of social inequality and social differentiation that makes it unlike its richer OECD partners.

Burgeoning Economic Growth has also Come with Economic Downsides

When grouped into distinct time periods – coinciding with notable landmarks in Chile's recent political history – the economic statistics show some interesting features that shed light on the neoliberal paradigm and Chile's application of it. The overriding impression is that adhering strictly to macroeconomic fundamentals is *not* enough to ensure steady, high-end economic growth when sector-specific weaknesses are not addressed.

1940–1985 versus 1986–2009: Chile's Growth has Performed Much More Strongly in the Past Twenty-Five Years

Chile's economic growth path reached a turning point in the second half of the 1980s, when the growth rate accelerated markedly in comparison with its historical record of the 1940–85 period (Figure 4.1 and Table 4.1). GDP grew in 1986–2009 by an average of nearly 5.4 percent annually,

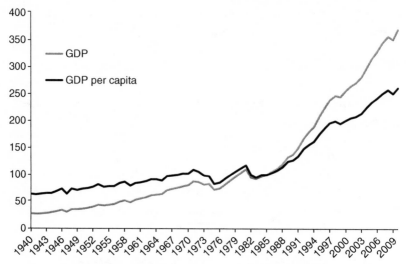

Figure 4.1 Real GDP level and per capita index, 1985 = 100.
Source: Author's elaboration based on data from Díaz, Lüders, and Wagner (2007) and the Central Bank of Chile.

in contrast to an annual growth rate of only 3.1 percent in 1940–85. Figure 4.1 displays the evolution of total GDP and GDP per capita for a period of near seventy years, running from 1940 to 2009. Some features of the growth process during this long period can be highlighted thus:

a) Steady though not spectacular growth from 1940 to 1970.
b) Under the Allende government (1970–3), growth initially accelerated but then declined but not dramatically.
c) Pinochet's neoliberal policies, launched in the mid-1970s, were followed by very volatile growth and sharp cycles as also shown in Figure 4.2. In fact, Chile experienced two big recessions, in 1975 and 1982–3, with GDP declining by 13 percent in 1975 and more than 16 percent in 1982–3. Between those two recessions, there was a relatively strong but ultimately short-lived recovery.
d) Adjustment policies supported by generous loans from multilateral financial institutions in Washington, DC in 1983–4 helped growth return by 1985.
e) Growth began its steady climb in the second half of the 1980s but was interrupted by the recession of 1999, in the aftermath of the Russian/East Asian crisis and again by the recession of 2009

Table 4.1. *Chilean Economic Growth and Enabling Factors: A Comparison between 1940–1985 and 1986–2009*

	1940–1985	1986–2009	1986–1997	1998–2009
Growth Indicators				
Real GDP Growth (% Annual Change)	3.1	5.4	7.6	3.3
Real Per Capita Growth Rate (% Annually)	1.2	4.0	5.8	2.1
Standard Deviation of GDP Growth	6.1	3.2	2.4	2.3
Population Growth (% Annually)	2.0	1.4	1.7	1.1
Gross Fixed Capital Formation (% of GDP)	14.3	21.9	22.8	21.1
Gross National Savings (% of GDP)	16.4	22.2	22.7	21.7
Total Factor Productivity (Index 1960 = 100)	102.8	107.5	102.7	112.9
Exports of Goods and Services (% of GDP)	16.5	33.7	29.8	37.5
Terms of Trade (Jan. 1997 = 100)	125.1	120.8	98.4	143.2
Macroeconomic Indicators				
Fiscal Balance (% of GDP)	−1.3	1.7	1.9	1.5
Inflation Rate (% Annual Change)	38.3	8.9	14.5	3.4
Current Account Balance (% of GDP)	−4.6	−1.4	−3.0	0.2
Real Exchange Rate Index (index 2000 = 100)	147.1	111.3	114.7	108.0
Employment & Labor Indicators				
Unemployment Rate (% Annually)	13.3	8.5	8.1	8.9
Real Wages (Index 2000 = 100)	66.8	92.3	77.5	107.1
Real Wages (% Annual change)	–	2.9	3.6	2.2

Sources: Díaz, Lüders, and Wagner (2007); Central Bank of Chile; DIPRES; and INE. Some data in Column 2 starts in 1960.

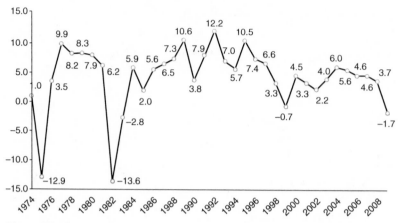

Figure 4.2 Chile – Growth swings in 1974–2009 (GDP constant prices, annual percentage changes).
Source: Author's elaboration based on data from Central Bank of Chile.

following the global financial crisis of 2008–9. Average growth was 7.6 percent per year in 1986–97 and declined to 3.3 percent in 1998–2009 (see Figure 4.2 for the dynamics of growth rates).

f) Growth volatility has declined in the past twenty-five years. In fact, the standard deviation in 1940–85 was 6.1, going down to 2.4 in the high growth period of 1986–97 and then to 2.3 in 1998–2009.

The acceleration in economic growth in the past two decades – the real measure of the so-called economic miracle of Chile[1] – reflects two broad factors underlying the policy climate of Chile's post-Pinochet democracy. One is the favorable effect of macroeconomic, social, and political stability (a socioeconomic "peace" not seen in decades), although some attribute this to a largely "dormant" society. The other is the effect of the private sector's strong response to the combination of market incentives and a substantial exposure to external markets, helped by a demobilized labor movement that provided "well-behaved," inexpensive labor to the production sector. In addition, an increased demand for investment due to the

---

[1] Fuentes et al. (2006), De Gregorio (2004), and Solimano (2006) all provide detailed analyses of Chile's growth path.

opportunities of external opening and internal market liberalization in the recent period has been matched by an increase in national savings that has been made possible by more developed capital markets, providing greater capacity to mobilize overall savings to match investment. These growth dynamics seem to fit better with investment-led growth models.[2] The external trade environment (terms of trade and foreign demand) experienced various cycles during this period, with relatively strong demand in the 1990s and 2000s, although punctuated, as mentioned before, by the Asian and Russian crisis in the late 1990s and the financial crisis of the late 2000s in the United States and Europe (the latter preceded by very high real copper prices, the main export of Chile).[3] What supply-and-demand factors (savings, investment, exports, and productivity) were at work in the acceleration of economic growth in Chile since the mid- to late-1980s? A summary list follows:[4]

1. An increase of 7.6 percentage points of GDP in gross fixed capital formation from 1986 to 2009, compared with the 1940–85 historical period.

---

[2] See Solimano and Gutierrez (2009).

[3] In the recession of 2009, total Chilean exports fell by around 19 percent, with the major declines concentrated in industrial and agricultural exports.

[4] Some of the features of the economic context under which growth unfolded during the past twenty-five years are worth mentioning. In the second half of the 1980s, the Chilean economy still had unused capacities as it was recovering from a major economic contraction earlier in the decade. In turn, the economy was affected after 1998 by the Asian and Russian crises, and growth remained sluggish for nearly five years after the onset of the crises (the growth record of the Lagos administration of 2000–6 was not spectacular). Economic growth accelerated in 2004–8 but not in proportion to the sharp rise in copper prices. As we already pointed out in Chapter 2, Chile seems to be a special case in which the strong terms-of-trade boom of the preglobal financial crisis period did not translate into faster economic growth – an anomaly that may be due in part to a fiscal policy dedicated to saving most of the terms-of-trade bonanza (nearly US$20 billion dollars by 2008, deposited abroad mostly in U.S. banks, as part of its Stabilization Fund, and nearly US$23 billion held by the central bank in international reserves in the same period). Fiscal policy followed a rule in which the government was to maintain a fiscal surplus above a certain percentage of GDP. In fact, the government ran a (current) fiscal surplus of 7.7 percent of GDP in 2006 and 8.2 percent of GDP in 2007 and, consequently, put itself in a very favorable fiscal position, particularly in U.S. dollars. The Chilean public sector became a net creditor in dollars and maintains a small internal public debt (central-government gross debt declined from 45 percent of GDP in 1990 to 6.1 percent of GDP in 2009).

2. An increase of around 6 percentage points of GDP in national savings in both periods, with a significant contribution of private savings that came mainly from the business and public sectors.
3. Acceleration in total factor productivity growth (or the efficiency with which productive resources are being used in the economy).[5]
4. A steady rise in the export share of GDP, which doubled from 1986 to 2009, compared with the historical reference period of 1940–85.

Although we wait until a latter section of this chapter for a more in-depth discussion, the following macroeconomic indicators also supported the growth performance of the last twenty to twenty-five years:

- A steady overall decline in inflation.
- A shift from fiscal deficits to fiscal balance and surpluses.
- A lower reliance on external savings and a cut in current account deficits in the balance of payments.

As was shown earlier in Figure 4.1 and Table 4.1, per capita GDP has also risen quite dramatically in the past twenty-five years compared with the earlier historical period: 4.0 percent annual growth versus only 1.2 percent in 1940–85. This increase in per capita income growth should have made a vast difference in the living standards of the average Chilean citizen. In fact, under the neoliberal era, per capita income growth throughout the world has not generally translated into broader-based economic welfare and security for the average citizen, i.e., the middle class, let alone the working poor. This is no truer than in Chile, where a middle class remains such a fuzzy concept, because the income distribution is so skewed toward the top.[6] More rapid economic growth in Chile has also meant that income inequality has not declined. In turn, wealth distribution is even more concentrated than income distribution, driven by the concentration of ownership in financial assets, productive wealth, and land (see Chapter 7).[7] At the same time, and as we will see in the next chapter, rapid economic growth (in conjunction with targeted social transfers)

---

[5] Fuentes, Larraín and Schmidt-Hebbel (2006) provide an analysis of the evolution of total factor productivity growth.
[6] See Solimano (2008) for a cross-country analysis of the middle class.
[7] Davies et al. (2006) provide international evidence on this facet of inequality.

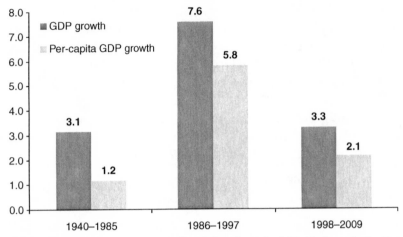

Figure 4.3 Chile – GDP growth has fallen from its historical marks in the 1986–1997 period (Total and per capita GDP, average annual percentage changes).
Source: Author's elaboration based on data from Díaz, Lüders, and Wagner (2007) and Central Bank of Chile.

has reduced *official* poverty in the past twenty years, from more than 45 percent in the late 1980s to approximately 15 percent in 2009.[8]

We make mention of this nexus between poverty reduction and the combination of income inequality and a middle-class standard of living in Chile as a cautionary tale for interpreting the statistics we discuss in this chapter. In the next chapter, we discuss this nexus in much more detail.

The 1986–1997 and 1998–2009 Periods: Economic Growth has Dropped off in the Twelve-Year-Period

The growth dynamics of the past twenty-five years has not been uniform across the two subperiods (1986–97 and 1988–2009), with a significant deceleration in total GDP and per capita GDP growth rates experienced since the late 1990s and through the 2000s compared with the rapid growth of the period 1986–97 (see Table 4.1 and Figure 4.3). In fact, average GDP growth in the 1986–97 subperiod was more than double that

---

[8] As mentioned already in Chapter 1, according to Larraín (2008) this decline in poverty is overstated by the official statistics for 2000, 2003 and 2006 (see also Chapter 5).

of the 1998–2009 period (7.6 percent annually versus only 3.3 percent, or 3.7 percent without including the recession year 2009). It is worth noting that the average rate of total GDP growth in 1998–2009 is closer to the average rate of 1940–85 (3.3 percent and 3.1 percent, respectively). GDP per capita growth, however, still accelerated by 1 percentage point per year in the 1998–2009 period compared with the historical reference years 1940–85. This suggests that an important part of the increase in per capita GDP of the later period is because of a lower population growth rate than a significant increase in total GDP growth.

Chilean Growth in International Perspective

An international comparison between economic growth in Chile and growth in other countries shows that Chile's GDP grew faster, on average, than other countries in the Latin American region in the 1987–98 period (Table 4.2). In the 2000s, however, this growth leadership started to fade away, and countries such as Colombia, Dominican Republic, and Peru managed to grow faster than Chile (this comparison holds also for per capita GDP). Still, Chile grew in this period faster than such large Latin American countries as Argentina, Brazil, and Mexico. The decline in the leading growth position of Chile with respect to the Latin American region coincides with a deceleration in growth in the 2000s, as well as the acceleration in growth rates in several of the competitor countries. In turn, if we compare the growth performance of Chile with respect to emerging economies outside the Latin America and Caribbean region, we note that in the past twenty years (1990–2009), Chilean growth has been behind fast-growing economies such as those in China, India, Malaysia, Singapore, South Korea, and Ireland (see Table 4.2).

Chilean Growth: Resource and Environmental Sustainability

Sir John Hicks, the famous British economist, maintained that sustainable real income (and thus sustainable growth trajectories) is one in which future generations are not impaired by savings and investment decisions made in the present. This concept is relevant to evaluating the sustainability of Chilean growth, particularly given its excessive reliance on natural resources (renewable and nonrenewable), its high energy use, its high geographical and proprietary concentration of

Table 4.2. *Economic Growth in Chile and Emerging Economies, 1987–
2009 (Annual Rate of Change, Percentages)*

	GDP Growth			Per Capita GDP Growth		
	1987–1998	1990–2009	2000–2009	1987–1998	1990–2009	2000–2009
Chile	7.4	5.0	3.7	5.6	3.6	2.6
Botswana	8.1	4.9	3.8	5.2	2.8	2.2
China	9.9	10.1	10.3	8.6	9.2	9.6
India	5.7	6.4	7.1	3.7	4.6	5.5
Indonesia	5.7	5.0	5.1	4.0	3.5	3.8
South Korea	6.8	5.3	4.4	5.8	4.6	3.9
Malaysia	7.6	6.0	4.8	4.7	3.7	2.8
Singapore	8.3	6.6	5.6	5.1	3.8	3.2
Argentina	3.1	3.8	3.6	1.7	2.5	2.4
Brazil	2.0	2.5	3.3	0.3	1.1	2.1
Colombia	3.8	3.4	4.0	2.0	2.0	2.8
Dominican Republic	5.0	5.1	5.1	3.0	3.4	3.6
Mexico	3.1	2.6	1.9	1.3	1.2	0.8
Peru	1.6	4.2	5.1	−0.4	2.6	3.8
Greece	1.8	2.7	3.4	1.1	2.2	3.2
Ireland	6.3	5.5	3.9	5.9	4.2	2.2
Italy	2.0	1.0	0.5	1.9	0.7	0.0
Portugal	3.4	2.0	0.9	3.3	1.7	0.5
Russia*	-	3.8	5.5	-	4.1	5.7
Spain	3.3	2.8	2.6	3.1	1.9	1.2

*Data since 1996.
Sources: WDI, World Bank, EUROSTAT, National Statistics.

productive assets, and the environmental implications of its export
base. Critical questions that must be addressed by any current and
future government are the following:

Can Natural-Resource Use Continue to be
Sustained as an Export Base?

It is estimated that around 70 percent of Chilean exports (more
than 35 percent of GDP) rely on raw materials and processed natural resources: copper, fruits, fishmeal, timber, and others. For a country that seeks to grow at an average rate of 6 percent annually (to
reach "development"), after the already relatively rapid growth for

Table 4.3. *Chile: Not Enough Progress is Being Made Toward Clean Energy, 2006–2010 (Sources of Energy Generation, Percentages)*

Source	2006	2007	2008	2009	2010
Hydroelectric	52.5	39.7	41.9	43.4	36.5
Coal, Oil	23.6	48.5	51.3	46.1	42.0
Natural Gas	23.9	11.7	6.8	10.4	20.9
Wind Power	0.0	0.0	0.1	0.1	0.6
Total	100	100	100	100	100

Source: Energy National Commission, CNE.

more than two decades under this strategy, the pressures on natural resources and the environment can be significant.[9]

Can Energy-Intensive Growth be Sustained?

A joint evaluation undertaken by the OECD with ECLAC (OCDE and CEPAL, 2005) on the environmental and energy consequences of rapid growth in Chile warns that this process is significantly increasing the intensity of Chilean energy consumption (the GDP growth-energy elasticity is above unity). Most expert analysts warn of the huge need to generate adequate electricity if the Chilean economy is to grow at 6 percent per year for a decade or so. Of course, how this electricity is generated is critical for the environment and for the quality of life of populations living in areas close to energy-generation plants. According to the Chile's National Energy Commission (see Table 4.3 below) in 2010, the main sources of electricity generation were coal and oil, followed by hydroelectric. In contrast, in 2006 the main source of electricity generation was hydroelectric. The share of wind-based electricity generation is very low, a surprising feature for a country with more than 3,000 miles of coastline. Also, the use of solar energy is nil.

Can the Environment Continue to Withstand Rapid Growth?

The consequences of rapid economic growth for the environment are quite serious, as highlighted in the OECD/ECLAC report. Resources devoted to prevention and mitigation of such consequences are still limited. Rapid growth in GDP and consumption have a variety of direct effects on the environment – an increase in fossil-fuel emissions

[9] Sunkel (1994) provides an early analysis of the pressure of rapid growth on water resources, energy, forestry, and the environment in Chile.

and other pollutants, an intensive use of energy to meet consumption demands, the exploitation of water, soil, and forestry resources, the rapid extraction of sea products and aggressive mining, and overcongestion in urban areas associated with a sharp increase in the stock of cars and transport vehicles.

Chile as a Leader in Orthodox Macroeconomics

During the past twenty-five years, the strong policy consensus in Chile has been that economic growth is predicated on ensuring macroeconomic stability – low inflation, low fiscal deficits, and moderate current account deficits. The underlying view was that a sufficient condition for growth to proceed was to have a stable macroeconomics framework. Industrial policy was seen as unnecessary or, worse, unproductive. This principle was, of course, an underlying message of the Washington Consensus, a message that was highly influential in Chile. Although the Concertación governments adopted some variations of the orthodoxy of the Consensus, mainly in the 1990s (such as taxes on capital inflows, managed exchange rates, and gradual disinflation), the economic teams of the socialist presidents of the 2000s embraced that same orthodoxy when they assumed leadership positions in the democratic governments.

The importance of macroeconomic conditions was amply demonstrated in the Chilean case. In fact, the country suffered the trauma of fiscal and inflationary crises in the 1970s and currency devaluation and financial collapse in the early 1980s, which interrupted economic growth and caused a huge surge in unemployment, a decline in real wages, and deterioration in human welfare. Since then, the four Concertación administrations gave central priority to macroeconomic management and performance over inequality and environmental goals. In turn, Chile followed or even anticipated the orthodoxy of the times regarding macroeconomic management. In the late 1980s, at the end of the Pinochet regime and with the agreement of the opposition of the time, Chile established an independent central bank with the mandate of ensuring low and stable inflation and normalcy in internal and external payments.[10] Thus, the main policy objective of

---

[10] See Blanchard et al. (2010) and Solimano et al. (2010) for reassessments of the macroeconomic orthodoxy of the 1990s and 2000s regarding central-bank policy and fiscal policy in light of the financial crisis of 2007–9 in advanced economies.

the central bank is to ensure low inflation. Steady GDP growth, full employment, and the maintenance of an "adequate," stable exchange rate is not included as policy objectives according to the constitutional charter of the Chilean central bank. This is certainly different from the objectives of the central banks of several advanced economies, most notably the U.S. Federal Reserve. Over time, however, managing inflation became the sole policy objective of several central banks in both advanced and emerging economies, a sign of the influence of orthodoxy that reached central banks around the world, a stance now shattered after the crisis of 2008–9.[11] In turn, the independent Central Bank of Chile as guardian of monetary stability was to be shielded from political pressures.[12] In line with the independent status of the bank, its top authorities (the governor and board members) were appointed for ten years. The president and the board of the bank form a small elite of public officials enjoying superstable and well-paid jobs that make important decisions (with various distributive effects) that affect the course of the economy and the welfare of various economic agents with their decisions.

The macroeconomic policies of the 1990s were gradualist on the anti-inflationary front, the exchange-rate regime was "managed" (under an adjustable-exchange-rate band) until 1999, and fiscal policy was generally prudent but without an explicit fiscal rule (until 2000). Taxes to deter short-term capital inflows were used until 2000, when they were removed and floating exchange rates were adopted. In the late 1990s, Chile moved to flexible exchange rates. The macroeconomic indicators of the period can be observed in Table 4.4 (drawn from earlier Table 4.1).

In the 2000s, macroeconomic policies imposed rules. This was probably a pioneer move in the Latin American context but was also a fashionable recommendation in the academic macroeconomics in the north. Of course, political economy decisions relevant to Chile were also considered. The rules were in the conduct of fiscal policy (see

---

[11] Of course, monetary authorities cannot be completely oblivious to the real cycles of the economy, nor to the effects of their own policies on the intensity and timing of these cycles. In Chile, central-bank authorities must report to parliament each year on the march of the economy.

[12] Although it is obvious central banks are the object of influence by governments and the powerful commercial bank community always sensitive to the interest-rate and exchange-rate decisions of the monetary authorities.

Table 4.4. *Chile: Macroeconomic Performance, 1945–2009*

Selected Variables	1940–1985	1986–2009	1986–1997	1998–2009
Fiscal Balance (% of GDP)	−1.3	1.7	1.9	1.5
Inflation Rate (% Annual Change)	38.3	8.9	14.5	3.4
Current Account Balance (% of GDP)	−4.6	−1.4	−3.0	0.2
Real Exchange Rate Index (2000 = 100)	147.1	111.3	114.7	108.0

Source: See Table 4.1.

below). The central bank, in turn, adopted the policy of "inflation targeting" – a practice that after the financial crisis of 2008–9 has come under criticism in other places of the world. In turn, to the extent possible, the central bank was to refrain from intervening in the foreign-exchange market.[13] It was apparent that rules replaced discretion as the new conventional wisdom, although the central bank used discretion, for example in the event of sharp appreciations or depreciations of the exchange rate.

Let us look at these policies in greater detail. Table 4.5 provides an overview of the macroeconomic policies adopted by Presidents Aylwin, Frei, Lagos, and Bachelet, who constitute the four Concertación administrations.

Fiscal Policy: Running a Structural Surplus
In 2000, the Lagos administration, following the advice of the budget director and the minister of finance, formalized a fiscal rule that the government was to run a structural fiscal surplus as a certain percentage of GDP (the administration set the mark at 1 percent). The purpose of the move was to make fiscal policy more predictable and to

---

[13] The central bank has intervened in the foreign-exchange market on very few occasions. Once in 2001 and associated with both the instability created by September 11 and the crisis of the Argentinean currency board; and again in 2002, after turbulence linked to the Brazilian elections. In turn, it opened a program of purchasing U.S. dollars to avoid a sharp appreciation of the peso in 2008 before the onset of the global financial crisis in the months before the U.S. financial crisis in September 2008. The last intervention occurred at the beginning of 2011 (with daily purchases of US$50 million) amid strong Chilean economic growth, record copper prices, and global U.S. dollar depreciation.

Table 4.5. *Chile: Main Macroeconomic Policies, 1990–2009*

	Aylwin Administration (1990–1994)	**Frei Administration (1994–1999)**	**Lagos Administration (2000–2005)**	**Bachelet Administration (2006–2009)**
Fiscal Policy	Austere (without fiscal rule)	Moderately austere (without fiscal rule)	Rule of structural fiscal surplus: 1% of GDP	Rule of structural fiscal surplus: 0.5% of GDP (from 2007)
Exchange Rate Policy	Exchange rate band	Exchange rate band	Floating	Floating
Monetary Policy	Eclectic	Eclectic	Inflation targeting	Inflation targeting
Taxes to Short-Term Capital Flows	Yes	Yes	No	No

Sources: Author's elaboration and Solimano and Pollack (2006).

forestall possible pressures on fiscal spending coming from political parties, parliamentarians, interest groups, and others, thus reducing the degree of discretion in fiscal spending and forcing increases in public spending to be aligned with what were considered to be permanent rises in copper prices, potential GDP, and other sources of revenue. Thus, cyclical improvement in terms of trade or transitory increases in tax revenues owing to faster economic growth are not to trigger proportional or more than proportional increases in public spending, often considered a main source of macroeconomic imbalances and unsustainable cycles in Latin America. The new 2000 rule demanding a structural fiscal surplus of 1 percent of GDP (later, the Bachelet administration reduced the specific value of the structural surplus to 0.5 percent of GDP) was predicated on the structural budget, which is calculated on the basis of medium-term projections of the main sources of fiscal revenue, often calculated by government-appointed committees of experts who struggle to get, with some scientific pretense, the medium-run price of copper and potential GDP, two parameters not easy to determine.[14]

[14] In August 2006 a Law of Fiscal Responsibility was approved that provides a legal framework to the policy of structural fiscal balances. The law authorizes the creation of wealth sovereign funds and allows the recapitalization of the central bank. See www.dipres.cl/572/articles-41380_doc_pdf.pdf.

The rule is also consistent with some degree of countercyclical fiscal policy, since it allows the government to run deficits in years when GDP is below full capacity, to be financed by the assets accumulated in surplus years. For example, the fiscal surplus was 7.7 percent of GDP in 2006, 8.2 percent in 2007, and 4.3 percent in 2008. In 2009, the budget ran a deficit of 4.5 percent of GDP. The extent of countercyclical polices in the past decade, however, is open to debate. For example, aggregate demand polices in 2000–3 were mildly countercyclical despite favorable conditions for accelerating a recovery of growth and employment at a time of low inflation, existing unused capacity, and access to external borrowing at low cost. In turn, the dramatic surge in copper prices since 2006 was not followed by an acceleration in GDP growth. At the same time, President Bachelet was able to put $1 billion of the bonanza saved by the government back into the economy as home and business loans and credit when the economic crisis of 2009 first hit and to launch a fiscal stimulus package that cost US$4 billion in 2009. As a result of Chile's favorable fiscal position, particularly in U.S. dollars, the Chilean public sector became a net creditor in dollar terms and has been able to maintain a small internal public debt: gross public debt declined from 45 percent of GDP in 1990 to 6.2 percent in 2009. In turn, net public sector debt was -20.4 percent of GDP in 2008 and declined to −11.2 percent in 2009 as the government used accumulated assets in the Economic Stabilization Fund to finance the fiscal deficit of 2009 (see Table 4.6 in footnote below).[15]

---

[15] Table 4.6. *Gross and Net Central Government Debt (% of GDP)*

Year	Gross Debt	Net Debt	Period
1990	44.8	32.1	Back to democracy
1998	12.7	−0.5	Economic crisis
1999	13.9	1.6	
2005	7.3	−0.1	Copper boom
2006	5.3	−7.0	
2007	4.1	−13.7	
2008	5.2	−20.4	
2009	6.2	−11.2	Economic crisis

Source: Budget office, DIPRES.

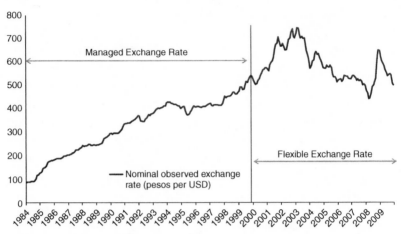

Figure 4.4 Chile – Evolution of the nominal exchange rates under two exchange rate systems, 1984–2010.
Source: Central Bank of Chile.

Exchange-Rate Policy: Still Grappling with Exchange-Rate Fluctuations

Since September 1999, Chile has operated under a system of floating exchange rates that replaced the "adjustable band (managed)" system of the 1990s. The regimen of an adjustable band proved to be complicated to manage as persistent capital inflows during most of the 1990s (until 1997), exerted "downward" pressure on the exchange rate (to appreciate), moving the market exchange rate to the floor of the band (Figure 4.4). The central bank engaged in expensive sterilization operations to counteract the monetary effect of massive purchases of foreign exchange. In 1998–9, a tight monetary policy was complemented by one to reduce exchange-rate flexibility (a move that narrowed the band, reducing the distance between the floor and the ceiling of the band) in the face of adverse terms-of-trade shocks and a decline in capital inflows. The policy was surprising because, in general, responding to adverse external shocks that cannot be financed fully requires more (not less) exchange-rate flexibility and often a depreciation of the real exchange rate. Since 2005, the exchange rate has shown a strong tendency to appreciate (again, see Figure 4.4), and the central bank in general tried to refrain from intervening in the foreign-exchange market, in spite of pressures from exporters and import-competing sectors that identified the policy of a strong peso

Table 4.7. *Chile: Volatility of the Nominal Exchange Rate, 1989–2010*

	1989–1999	2000–2010
ST Deviation Of:		
Monthly Variation	1.5	2.9
Yearly Variation	6.7	12.6

Source: Author's elaboration based on data from Central Bank of Chile.

as undermining the competitiveness of Chilean industry and agriculture. The policy of nonintervention in the foreign-exchange market, however, was not always possible to sustain. In early 2008, the nominal exchange rate (peso/dollar) appreciated by more than 10 percent in nominal terms in the face of high copper prices, a weak dollar in international currency markets, and the Chilean government's strong dollar fiscal surplus. In the face of a sharp appreciation of the peso, the central bank decided to intervene between April and December 2008. Since September 2008, however, there was a sharp reversal of the value of the exchange rate: in late October 2008, the rate was nearly CLP (Chilean pesos) 670 per U.S. dollar, in comparison with March 2008, when the exchange rate was CLP 440 per U.S. dollar.

Thus, the experience of flexible exchange rates without intervention in the 2000–10 period has been one of large fluctuations in the nominal exchange rate. As shown in Table 4.7, the standard deviation of the nominal exchange rate variation almost doubled between 2000–10 compared with the period 1989–99 (both using month-to-month and year-to-year changes).

The policy of the Chilean central bank since the inception of flexible exchange rates has been one of minimal intervention as already noted. It is an open question, however, as to the extent to which the volatility of the exchange rate just mentioned could have been reduced had the central bank followed a more interventionist stance.

The attendant dilemma is that an undisturbed market equilibrium (with the central bank watching the market but refraining from intervening) may yield an exchange-rate level that is misaligned,[16]

---

[16] The concept of "exchange-rate equilibrium" in itself is tricky, but as a reasonable approximation its determinants include the terms of trade, capital inflows, productivity growth, and other variables.

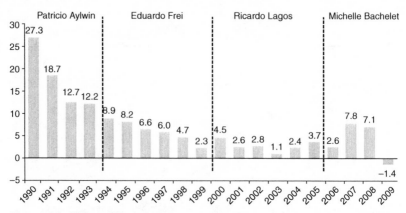

Figure 4.5 Chile – The inflation rate under four *concertación* governments, 1990–2009 (CPI, average annual percentage change).
Source: Author's elaboration based on data from Central Bank of Chile.

creating adverse real effects on economic activity and introducing uncertain price and profitability signals for export- and import-competing firms that create jobs and are the engine for growth in Chile.[17]

Monetary Policy: The Overriding Objective of the Central Bank to Keep Inflation in Check

In the past two decades, Chilean inflation was declining, with some variation across different years; a roughly similar process was seen in world inflation. In 1990, Consumer Price Index inflation was 27.3 percent (its highest peak since the onset of the 1981 recession), but by 2006 it fell to less than 3 percent. The next year, however, it accelerated to 7.8 percent, and in 2008 it was 7.1 percent in the wake of several food- and energy-price increases. In the recession year 2009, inflation turned negative, to −1.4, the first year of deflation in more than seven decades in Chile (see Figure 4.5). There is a controversy about the extent to which the shift to lower inflation worldwide (Chile included)

---

[17] The free-floating exchange-rate regime is credited to have led to: (1) a decline in "pass-through" coefficients between the exchange rate and prices that reduce the inflationary effect of currency depreciations; (2) small liability dollarization in the banking system, although the increased external indebtedness of the corporate sector reduces this effect; and (3) the creation of more sophisticated financial instruments to deal with exchange-rate fluctuations (De Gregorio and Tokman, 2004).

has been due to more zealous monetary authorities with little toler-
ance for inflation and/or the incorporation of more than one billion
new workers into the world economy (through international trade)
in China, India, the former Soviet Union, and other countries, moderating wage pressures and lowering the price of manufacturing goods.
Counteracting these anti-inflationary external trends is the increase
in oil and food prices, accelerating in 2008 and then again in 2010.
Another broad discussion on the objectives of the central banks is
the extent to which a concentrated focus on fighting inflation should
take preeminence over a more inclusive and nuanced macroeconomic
approach that includes a focus on full employment, financial stability,
and exchange rates.

Macroeconomic Policies and Performance under the *Concertación* Governments

A cursory examination of macroeconomic indicators across the four
Concertación administrations since 1990 seems to show clearly that
the neoliberal paradigm whereby economic growth is predicated on
macroeconomic austerity does not hold true in Chile, at least without
qualifications (Table 4.8). Obviously, as we note in the text, a variety of external factors in the global community can affect whether
any economy grows and at what pace. But in Chile, the macroeconomic orthodoxy of fiscal rules, inflation targeting, no taxes on capital inflows and market-determined exchange rates have not led to
dynamic and sustained economic growth that has filtered down into
job creation, lower unemployment, and real wage gains. In particular, the period of higher inflation of the 1990s was accompanied by
higher average growth than the lower inflation period of the orthodox decade of the 2000s.

GDP growth was the highest during the Aylwin administration
(averaging 7.7 percent annually from 1990 to 1994). Average annual
growth during the Frei administration was 5.4 percent (1994–9), followed by the Lagos administration (averaging 4.3 percent annually
from 2000 to 2005) and Bachelet (averaging 2.8 percent annually from
2006 to 2009). Per capita GDP growth was also lower during the Lagos
and Bachelet administrations than during the Aylwin and Frei governments. In turn, unemployment rates were higher during the socialist

Table 4.8. *Growth Performance and Macroeconomic Indicators across Centrist-Neoliberal Policies in the Four Administrations*

	P. Aylwin (1990–1993) Christian Democrat	E. Frei (1994–1999) Christian Democrat	R. Lagos (2000–2005) Socialist	M. Bachelet (2006–2009) Socialist
Growth Indicators				
Real GDP Growth Rate (% Annually)	7.7	5.4	4.3	2.8
Real Per Capita Growth Rate (% Annually)	5.8	3.9	3.1	1.8
Gross Fixed Capital Formation (% of GDP)	23.1	24.8	20.4	21.1
Gross National Savings (% of GDP)	24.2	22.6	20.9	23.3
Total Factor Productivity (1960 = 100)	101.1	112.8	113.4	112.0
Exports of Goods and Services (% of GDP)	30.4	27.9	36.2	44.2
Terms of Trade (Jan. 1997 = 100)	94.3	103.8	121.0	197.6
Macroeconomic Indicators				
Fiscal Balance (% of GDP)	1.9	1.2	0.6	3.9
Inflation Rate (% Annual Change)	17.7	6.1	2.9	4.0
Current Account Balance (% of GDP)	–2.3	–3.0	–0.2	2.3
Real Exchange Rate Index (2000 = 100)	120.2	98.1	111.8	109.7
Employment & Labor Indicators				
Unemployment Rate (% Annually)	7.3	7.3	9.7	8.1
Real Wages (Index 2000 = 100)	76.1	93.4	104.7	115.4
Real Wages (% Annual Change)	4.6	3.3	1.6	2.8

Source: See Table 4.1.

Lagos and Bachelet presidencies and real wages grew at slower rates than in the Aylwin and Frei governments.

One could be tempted to infer that the two Christian Democrat presidents managed to make the economy grow faster than the two Socialist presidents, but of course this different growth performance may not have a direct correspondence with the ideological affiliation of the presidents and may have more to do with the types of policies they implemented: it is apparent that Lagos and Bachelet were more ortho-dox in their economic policies than their predecessors regarding taxes on capital inflows, exchange-rate management, and inflation targeted by the central bank. Still, this growth performance – higher growth in the 1990s and lower growth in the 2000s – is puzzling given that the economy enjoyed on average more favorable terms of trade and lower inflation in the 2000s than in the 1990s. Yet inflation was highest during the high-growth Aylwin administration (averaging 17.7 percent annually) and lowest during the Lagos administration (averaging 2.9 percent annually), with higher inflation under Frei (6.1 percent annually) than under Bachelet (4.0 percent annually) amid external infla-tion shocks from food and oil commodities.

On the whole, fiscal policies were austere during the four Concertación governments, in line with the recommendation of the Washington Consensus for emerging economies (what the recom-mendations of the Bretton Woods institutions were to reduce the high fiscal deficits in the United States and the United Kingdom in the same period are unclear). The degree of fiscal austerity was particu-larly intense in the Bachelet government, when the bonanza in copper prices was largely saved, until 2008, in spite of the obvious needs for greater fiscal expenditure in social sectors (education, health, hous-ing, and pensions). The government insisted that austerity was the right policy to follow because it entailed precautionary savings for bad times. The bad times arrived in 2009, as GDP contracted by 1.7 percent in spite of countercyclical policies financed by previous fiscal savings. Under the fiscal rule adopted by the Lagos administration, the fis-cal deficit declined and then turned into large surpluses during the Bachelet administration. In general, all the Concertación administra-tions maintained moderate to low current-account deficits in the bal-ance of payments, which turned into surpluses in the record years of high copper prices, 2006–8.

Summing up, it is evident that the Concertación governments were quite mainstream in their macro policies (a stance that was also applied to social policy as shown in the next two chapters). Perhaps surprisingly, socialist presidents were more orthodox than their nonsocialist colleagues within the Concertación, with Lagos refraining from using fiscal, balance of payments spaces and low inflation to stimulate the economy in the early 2000s, and Bachelet's wanting to save the copper-price windfall of 2006–8 in spite of sluggish growth and accumulated social needs.

Concluding Remarks

In this chapter, we have documented the turning point in the growth dynamics of the Chilean economy that took place in the mid- to late 1980s, when the country started to accelerate its historical rate of GDP growth. The process over time led to a substantial increase in per capita GDP, to around US$14,000 in 2010. This growth performance, besides other policies, helped Chile get its membership to the OECD and claim a status of a country near the development stage. Looking into the dynamics of growth, it is apparent that this process has been uneven and accompanied by severe cycles in the last thirty-five years or so. These cycles were associated with the big recessions of 1975 and 1982–3 and the more moderate recessions of 1999 and 2009. These experiences of negative growth point to the propensity of the Chilean economy to experience the sudden stop of growth rates even when ample fiscal savings are available, as in 2009, that should theoretically allow a buffer for external shocks. In turn, the data show a decade- long trend toward slower economic growth since the late 1990s. The acceleration of growth of the 1990s was a story of investment-led growth supported by higher national savings and rapid exports expansion.

In terms of macroeconomic management, the governments of the 2000s championed an orthodoxy of independent central banks, fiscal rules, untaxed capital inflows, and flexible exchange rates (with only occasional intervention in the foreign-exchange market). The experience of economic growth and its relation to macroeconomic policies in the 1990s and 2000s defy simple associations between low inflation and fiscal deficits and growth performance. In fact, Chile grew faster in the 1990s when (moderate) inflation was higher but declining and the country had lower levels of fiscal savings and no fiscal rules, in apparent contrast with the basic tenets of conventional macroeconomics and its emphasis on "macroeconomic fundamentals" whose meaning and operational content is never quite precise.

5

The Social Record of the Post-Pinochet Administrations

Poverty Declines but High Inequality Persists

Introduction

In Chapter 4, we discussed Chile's economic progress under the four social-democratic administrations, with economic growth driven by exports and free markets and supported by "macroeconomic fundamentals." Despite achievements in macroeconomic performance and growth, the natural resource base is relied on too heavily, energy use is escalating, and environmental problems are mounting. Moreover, labor unions and social organizations had limited influence on policy formulation; and small and medium-size businesses are squeezed out of the export market. As the time of this book's completion, frustration with the education system and an unequal society has started to filter down into the social fabric of the country in the form of discontent and demands for social change, led by an active student movement.

What is particularly galling in Chile, however, is the persistence of income and wealth inequality nearly two decades after democracy was restored and in spite of (or perhaps supportive of) relatively high rates of economic growth that have provided a stronger economic resource base to finance social reforms. The Gini coefficient has remained virtually flat for the past twenty years, hovering around an unacceptable 55 percent, a number that probably *underestimates* effective inequality, because high incomes tend to be underreported in household surveys used to calculate the Gini. A large majority of the population has improved its living standards in the past two decades but still relatively moderately; in turn, this majority remains vulnerable to economic and nature shocks, has low levels of empowerment, and its influence in public policy is reduced. Targeted social policies have benefitted the very poor. A growing middle class, however, is still largely vulnerable to debt and faces fragile jobs and expensive social services. This middle class is entertaining new aspirations as it perceives that years of prosperity have largely been internalized by the economic elites, leaving other segments in society with little real empowerment.

Low priority given to public policies oriented to progressive income and wealth distribution not only by the Pinochet regime but also by the democratic administrations raises some intriguing questions about the nature of the relationship between democracy and equality. In fact, the Chilean experience shows that the transition from authoritarianism to democracy does not necessarily trigger a process of lower inequality. As mentioned before, the social priorities of the Chilean center-left – Christian Democrats and Socialists – have been insufficient to redress inequality now that the macroeconomic balances are under control and growth has remained positive (if not increasing), and they have stayed away from pro-equality policies, in sharp contrast to their historical stance on this issue.[1] The government coalition leaders probably still had fresh memories of the political turbulence and social conflict of the early 1970s in Chile, when redistributive policies were tried under the Allende government and fiercely opposed by the economic elites (and the administration of U.S. President Richard Nixon). Once they came to power, they avoided redistribution, focusing on the less politically contentious goal of reducing poverty. Reinforcing the point made earlier in Chapters 2 and 3, this was possible also because of the reduced capacities of those constituencies traditionally in favor of redistribution, such as grassroots social organizations and the labor movement, which were politically weak and fragmented.

The democratic governments of the past twenty years have aimed at improving social conditions and reducing social risk without really tackling the structural roots of inequality, which are driven by factors such as the high concentration of productive wealth and market shares, the existence of an education system that is strongly segmented by family income levels, the weak bargaining power of labor, and other factors we review in this chapter. In turn, the continuation of

---

[1] Part of the "traditional left" in Chile – the Communist Party – did not participate in any of the four democratic governments since 1990.

inequality mirrors the continuation of a system of political representation that emerged from the authoritarian regime and that has proved extremely difficult to modify (see Chapter 8).

The way different Concertación governments tried to approach social problems evolved over time. The antipoverty focus of the social policies of the 1990s– increased social spending – was complemented in the 2000s with policies of social protection aimed at reaching the middle class in which social benefits are backed by legislation following an approach of "social rights." Policies were intended to extend access to health and education to social groups such as the self-employed and independent producers. In turn, "universal" pensions were introduced that were financed by the state. An unemployment insurance scheme (of limited coverage that reaches only workers in the formal private sector) was also created, and several changes were introduced to various social programs. These social reforms of the 2000s, however, did not affect in any significant way the system of profit-oriented AFPs (private administrators of pension funds) and profit-oriented ISAPRES (private health service providers); they also did not address the deterioration in public education and the lack of funding for public universities, a key mechanism for equalizing opportunities. The private providers of social services constitute powerful interest groups almost immune to effective regulation and competition from the state. These issues are touched on in greater depth in Chapter 6.

Declining Poverty: Yes, but to What Extent?

Chile has been portrayed as an almost textbook case of successful growth-led poverty reduction helped by targeted social policies: the role model any middle-income country should look to for guidance and inspiration. The numbers show that an increase in per capita income associated with more rapid growth led to a decline in poverty from 45 percent in 1987 to 15.1 percent in 2009 (Table 5.1). In turn, acute poverty declined from 17.4 percent in 1987 to 3.7 percent in 2009. The decline in poverty was sustained from 1987, but a small increase took place in 2009 (the last year of the CASEN survey), which was probably associated with the recession of that year among other factors. The significant reduction in poverty is generally explained by the combination of reasonably rapid growth and targeted social programs,

Table 5.1. *Chile: Official Poverty Shows a Drastic Decline,*
1987–2009

Year	Poverty Rate (%)	Acute Poverty Rate (%)
1987	45.1	17.4
1990	38.6	12.9
1992	32.6	8.8
1994	27.5	7.6
1996	23.2	5.7
1998	21.7	5.6
2000	20.6	5.7
2003	18.8	4.7
2006	13.7	3.2
2009	15.1	3.7

Source: CASEN surveys (1987–2009).

suggesting a confirmation of the importance attached to growth as a critical condition for improving social conditions and reducing poverty (but not necessarily inequality). The actual level of poverty in Chile, however, was questioned in a study by the economist Felipe Larraín (Larraín, 2008).[2]

Table 5.2 presents the differences between the incidence of poverty calculated in Larraín (2008) and official poverty for the years 2000, 2003, and 2006. The differences in poverty levels are very significant: the recalculated poverty levels fall fifteen to eighteen points *higher* than the official rate for the three years indicated above. In particular, the study arrives at a poverty rate of 29 percent in 2006, which is more than double the official rate of 13.7 percent. In turn, critical (acute) poverty is also higher: 6.2 percent versus 3.2 as reported officially.

Methodologically, Larraín (2008) updates the poverty line and generates a new consumption basket using a household consumption study of 1996–7, based on previous technical work conducted by Fundación para la Superación de la Pobreza.[3] The cost of the newly

---

[2] As of the beginning of 2011, Mr. Larraín is the finance minister in the government of President Sebastian Piñera.
[3] The Larraín study makes various adjustments to the composition of the basket using updated nutritional patterns, which arrive at a new Engel coefficient (2.26 for urban, 1.75 for rural). The new basket considers only Santiago owing to a lack of good data for the rest of the country.

Table 5.2. *Chile: Official and Recalculated Poverty for 2000, 2003, and 2006 (% of total)*

		2000	2003	2006
Acute Poverty	Official	5.6	4.7	3.2
	Larraín (2008)	10.4	9.6	6.2
	Difference	**4.8**	**4.9**	**3.0**
Total Poverty	Official	20.2	18.7	13.7
	Larraín (2008)	36.6	36.4	29.0
	Difference	**16.4**	**17.7**	**15.3**

Source: Own elaboration based on CASEN data and Larraín (2008).

computed basket is 51 percent higher than the cost of the official poverty line for 2006.

The official poverty line is based on the consumption patterns of the 1980s, which certainly do not reflect demographic changes (fertility, family size, urbanization) and economic changes (lower import duties, broader credit access, new goods, more public services, and other factors) that have occurred in the past two decades.[4]

The (Qualified) Success of Poverty Reduction – Though Not Assured – Should Now Give Way to Targeting Income Inequality

Thus, not only are the rapid declines in poverty still precarious, but the country also has not yet even begun to address its rampant, persistent income inequality. The numbers tell a dismal story for Chile (Table 5.3). As we mentioned, its Gini coefficient is one of the worst not just in the Latin American and Caribbean region but in the world (see Chapter 7 for some international comparisons). Although the decline in poverty is largely a by-product of the acceleration of growth – which was one of the tenets of the Washington Consensus – economic growth under the neoliberal model was also supposed to start spreading the wealth.

---

[4] Further, there was a change in nutritional recommendations for Chile by the FAO/WHO/UN, hence a change in minimum food requirements. These would mean new consumption habits and changes in the proportion of food expenditures to total expenditures (the Engel coefficient).

Table 5.3. *Chile: Persistent Inequality Makes Poverty Reductions a Pyrrhic Victory, 1987–2009*

Year	Gini for Autonomous Income (%)	Gini for Monetary Income (%)	Income Share for Top 10%	Income Share for Bottom 20%	Ratio of 10th to 1st Income Deciles
1987	58	58	47.4	3.2	37.6
1990	57	56	42.2	4.1	30.5
1992	56	56	41.8	4.3	28.1
1994	57	55	41.8	4.1	30.9
1996	57	56	41.8	3.9	33.0
1998	58	57	41.4	3.7	34.7
2000	58	58	42.7	4.0	34.2
2003	57	56	41.5	3.9	34.4
2006	54	53	38.6	4.1	31.3
2009	55	53	40.2	3.6	46.2

Source: CASEN surveys (1987–2009).

Despite the recent poverty reductions, however, evidence shows that the vulnerability to poverty is still a potential problem. In fact, it is estimated that nearly 30 percent of the population have incomes within 40 percent of the official poverty line (see Lopez and Miller, 2008), meaning that if a financial quake, even a tremor, occurs on the economic landscape, then a significant number of people could fall back into poverty. An example of that is the increase of a few percentage points in the share of population below the poverty line in 2009, a year of recession. Another major shock was the earthquake of February 27, 2010, which severely hit several provinces in Chile, particularly in the center-south of the country, leading to losses of human life, physical infrastructure, and housing. In fact, the adverse shocks of the economic crisis moved the percentage points of those in poverty back up.[5]

In Chile, income inequality seems not to have been affected by economic growth and by the higher level of GDP per capita. Chile is today much more affluent than two to three decades ago, but its inequality levels are similar if not worse. In contrast with the evolution

[5] Moreover, the exact number of people escaping poverty is sensitive to the definition of the poverty line. In Chile, poverty lines are on the basis of consumption shares recorded in the household surveys of the 1980s. Observers argue that this is a low poverty line (diminishing measured poverty).

Table 5.4. *Gini Coefficient: Selected Countries, 2000–2008*

Countries	%	Countries	%	Countries	%
South America		**Africa**		**Europe**	
Argentina	48.8	Congo, Dem. Rep.	44.4	Croatia	29.0
Brazil	55.0	Egypt	32.1	France	32.7
Chile	55.0	Ethiopia	29.8	Germany	28.3
Colombia	58.5	Ghana	42.8	Greece	34.3
Peru	50.5	Morocco	40.9	Hungary	30.0
Uruguay	47.1	Nigeria	42.9	Ireland	34.3
Venezuela	43.4	South Africa	57.8	Italy	36.0
Nordic Countries		Tanzania	34.6	Poland	34.9
Denmark	24.7	**Asia**		Romania	32.1
Finland	26.9	China	41.5	Russia	43.7
Norway	25.8	India	36.8	Spain	34.7
Sweden	25.0	Malaysia	37.9	Ukraine	27.6
North America		Thailand	42.5		
Canada	32.6	Turkey	41.2		
Mexico	51.6				
United States	40.8				

Source: World Development Report 2009, World Bank.

of poverty (despite the controversy on specific levels), the Gini coefficient remains persistently high. In fact, the Gini coefficient for autonomous income (that is, income earned in the market before subsidies and transfers from the government) remained virtually flat over the last 20 years, with a minor decline in 2006 and then a small increase in 2009. In turn, the Gini coefficient for total income – which includes the transfers and subsidies of the state – is slightly below the Gini for autonomous income. These Gini values are at the high end even for Latin America, a region already characterized by high inequality. As shown in Table 5.4, they are far higher than in the Scandinavian countries (with a Gini of 25–27 percent), North America, Africa (with the exception of South Africa), Asia, and Europe. Chilean Gini coefficients fall within the 10 percent of countries with the highest inequality levels in the world (this group includes Namibia, South Africa, Paraguay, Zimbabwe, and others with a Gini above 55 percent).

But the Gini coefficient is not the only evidence of income disparity. In 2006, the top 10 percent of the population in Chile captured

Panel A: Deciles

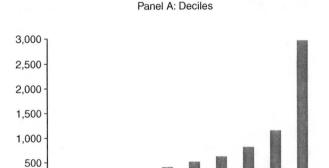

Panel B: Ventiles

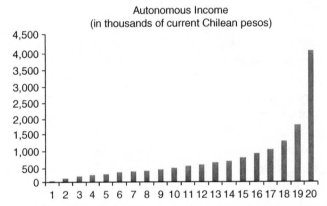

Figure 5.1 Chile – Income distribution – a steep slope down from the highest income groups (CASEN, 2009).

nearly 39 percent of income; in 2009, the disparity increased slightly to 40 percent. In contrast, the bottom 20 percent "captured" only 3.6 percent of income in 2009. These income inequality gaps cannot be overstated (Figure 5.1, panels A and B). In fact, it is apparent that income inequality in Chile is due primarily to the concentration of income at the top (that is, the richest 10 percent, 5 percent, and 1 percent) rather than acute poverty at the bottom of the distribution. And from the first to the ninth deciles, income distribution is relatively even, meaning that the disparity of income is much narrower. Thus, the main factor for income disparity is the very high income share of the top decile (10 percent partition) or ventile (5 percent partition) relative to the rest of the population.

The economic elites capture the lion's share of income generated in the economy. In fact, the values of the Gini coefficients for the complete distribution (from deciles one to ten) are significantly higher than the Gini for the deciles one to nine (Solimano and Torche, 2007). Indeed, if the top decile were excluded from the overall distribution, the resulting inequality levels would not be too different from the levels found in relatively more egalitarian countries (a Gini below 0.4).[6] Our measure of inequality focuses on income flows.

Growth, Poverty, and Inequality

The relationship between three critical variables – growth, poverty, and inequality in Chile for the period 1987–2009–is depicted in Figure 5.2. This chart shows a clear inverse relationship between poverty and GDP (growth leads to a decline in poverty), but the chart shows no discernable relationship between growth and income inequality proxy by the Gini coefficient. In short, growth seems not to lead to a decline in inequality, although it reduces poverty.

The Chilean experience of the past two decades illustrates the complexities and nuances of (a) the relationship between economic growth and social inequality and (b) the relationship between democracy and inequality (not shown in the graph).

The Resilience of Inequality during Growth

The Chilean experience of recent decades runs counter to modern political economy theories (as developed by Alesina and Rodrik [1994] and others authors) that predict a negative relationship between inequality and growth, with causality running from inequality to growth (higher

---

[6] See Solimano and Torche (2007). A mathematical note is relevant here: due to the formula of the Gini that includes several interaction terms, the total (or average) Gini coefficient for the whole distribution is not the average of the Gini for the individual subcomponents.

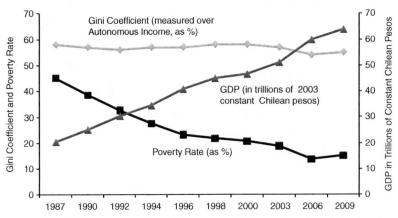

Figure 5.2 Chile – Growth and poverty have moved in the right direction but inequality remains high and flat, 1987–2009.
Source: Own elaboration based on data from CASEN surveys (1987–2009) and Central Bank of Chile.

inequality leads to slower economic growth, or in econometric terms, there is a negative coefficient of the inequality variable in growth equations).[7] A chief mechanism described in this literature highlighting a negative relationship between inequality and growth is increased polarization and social conflict associated with inequality. In the case of Chile, persistent inequality apparently did not harm growth in a significant way (and in turn, it was largely unaffected by growth itself, as shown in Figure 5.2); and social conflict between, say, labor and capital in the post-Pinochet period – so far – has not been acute. This is not the only possible sign, however, of the relationship between growth and inequality: older theories of savings-driven growth (for example, the Kaldor model, in which workers have a lower propensity to save than capitalists) predicted that a certain concentration of income distribution was necessary for boosting national savings needed to finance capital accumulation and spur growth. The Kaldor's theory suggested a positive relationship between inequality and growth (which was part of Kaldor's critique, namely that capitalist growth and income concentration went hand in hand). What remains puzzling is that high and

---

[7] See Solimano (1998) for a review and critical evaluation of various theories of growth and inequality.

stable Gini coefficients coexist with relatively rapid growth, suggesting that both variables (inequality and growth) may behave independently of each other.[8]

The Resilience of Inequality in a Democracy

Why did Chile's return to democracy (albeit with the limitations noted in this book) fail to lead to a decline in economic inequality? As in the relationship between growth and inequality, there are various possible theories of the relationship between democracy and inequality. One theory associated with the median-voters political economy theories is that in Chile voters had, after the return to democracy, a stronger preference for pro-growth policies than for pro-redistribution policies and accepted inequality as the price for more rapid growth. The fact is that the four Concertación governments were all pro-growth in their policies (for a while, the official mantra was "growth with equity") and they never really attempted a shift in income distribution away from rich economic elites (the coalition governed for twenty consecutive years before losing the presidency to a center-right coalition headed by Sebastian Piñera). The electoral support of the Concertación while it lasted gives empirical backing to the median-voter theory: that voters preferred pro-growth rather than pro-redistribution policies. This, however, may be just an after-the-fact rationalization, employing a theory that assumes the unrealistic capacity of common people (voters) to understand a very complex relationship among variables such as inequality, democracy, and growth – a relationship that even sophisticated economists do not agree on – in forming their political preferences. The theory also assumes that candidates and governments accommodate their electoral platforms to these allegedly sophisticated voters' preferences.

An alternative and more realistic interpretation is that the return to democracy in Chile did not lead to a decline in the power of capital (actually, as we shall see in Chapters 6 and 7, the economic power of capital has increased in the past two decades). The prevailing free-market, neoliberal model gives a privileged position to capital

---

[8] Solimano and Torche (2007) investigate this issue for Chile and note the degree of independence between both variables. See also Solimano (2009).

in setting the rules of the game in the economic system and shapes democracy accordingly.[9] In fact, it is apparent that the control of economic resources by powerful industrial, mining, banking, and other consortiums in Chile allows them to exert much more influence on public policy than other groups, such as labor unions, environmental groups, and student organizations. In particular, as already indicated, the labor movement has remained largely marginalized since the return of democracy, and its capacity to push for a shift in income distribution away from capital and profits toward labor and wage earners has been very weak. In addition, the dominating economic ideas of the left-wing coalition in power between 1990 and 2009 were, on the whole, close to the Washington Consensus that did not recommend egalitarian redistribution of income.

Conclusion: The Various Factors Explaining Persistent Inequality in Chile

The experience of the post-Pinochet transition shows the relative invariance and persistence of inequality in the face of the acceleration in economic growth and the advent of democracy. Several factors can account for its scale and persistence. These explanations combine the effects of globalization, concentration of productive wealth, quality segmentation between public and private education, lack of more progressive taxation, weak bargaining capacities of organized labor, and the low priority attached to reducing inequality in public policy making. The following is a list of these factors and influences:

- *Uneven access to the opportunities opened by globalization and liberalization policies.* The Chilean model is based on the integration of the national economy into external markets and the potential provided by globalization for wealth creation. Yet in a country with a differentiated social structure in terms of education, skills, and social connections, these opportunities tend to be captured by individuals with tertiary education levels, entrepreneurial drive, risk-taking attitudes, social connections, and access to credit. Because income levels are highly correlated with these factors, these gains

---

[9] Authors such as Kaletsky (2010), Marglin (2008), and Harvey (2010) elaborate on the power of capital in the neoliberal era prevailing since the 1980s.

tend to accrue disproportionately to entrepreneurial people and well-educated and well-connected individuals.[10]

- *Ownership in key sectors of Chile's economy is highly concentrated.* As mentioned before and explored in more detail in Chapter 7, the Chilean economy exhibits significant degrees of concentration in the ownership of productive capital and assets in banking, mining, manufacturing, retail trade, private pension-management companies (AFP), private health-care providers (ISAPRES), pharmacies, and other sectors with high rates of return per unit of invested capital. The supernormal profits generated in these sectors contribute to overall income inequality.

- *Significant differences in the quality of private and public school systems and thus unequal mechanisms for human capital accumulation and upward mobility.* In Chile, access to education is such that the children of the poor and middle class tend to attend public schools, whereas the children of the upper middle class and the rich go to semiprivate and private schools. Per-student resources in the public school system, however, are much lower than in private schools (a ratio of approximately one to four); this indicates that education is far from being an equalizing mechanism. On the contrary, it tends to replicate and reinforce other inequalities, in particular those of income and wealth.

- *The lack of more progressive taxation.* Another cause for the high levels of inequality in Chile is the low level of personal income taxation as share of total tax revenues of the state: 4.5 percent compared with an average of 25.2 percent in the OECD. Near half of total tax collection (48 percent) in Chile comes from indirect taxation, the value-added tax (see Table A.2 in the Annex). In turn, corporate tax rates, set transitorily at 19 percent for large corporations in 2010 after the earthquake, are low by Latin American

---

[10] A growing body of economic literature indicates that income and wealth inequality is closely related to the inequality of opportunity. This literature also highlights that inequality can harm growth by creating social polarization and political instability or, alternatively, can invite higher taxation, which is detrimental to investment. In addition, unequal societies suffer hidden economic losses because, given such constraints as a paucity of credit, limited information on opportunities, lack of social contacts, and restricted access to political power, many talented individuals belonging to less-favored or marginalized social groups are unable to realize their productive potential. See Solimano, Aninat, and Birdsall (2000).

standards, although similar to those in countries such as the Czech Republic, Poland, Hungary, and Slovakia.

- *A low level of worker unionization and the limited bargaining power of the working classes.* Organized labor was almost decimated during the military regime and never regained its pre-1973 strength and influence after the return to democracy in 1990. (Currently, unionization levels are around 12–14 percent.) The neoliberal model (with the high power of capital) and the competitive environment of globalization have led to flexible labor markets with low costs for hiring and, above all, firing workers. With weakened unions, labor has a limited role in setting wages and working conditions. Therefore, a weakened labor movement permanently threatened by the fear of unemployment, outsourcing, and the competition of immigrant labor is unable to capture a higher share of productivity gains (and national income) generated by a growing economy, affecting the functional distribution of income between capital and labor. This point was underscored by the classical economists David Ricardo and Karl Marx when discussing the determinants of functional income distribution in a capitalist economy.

- *An inclination by the successive post-Pinochet governments to ignore income inequality as part of their overall social agenda, which was largely dominated by poverty reduction.* Not only did the Pinochet regime neglect the income inequality issue (which would be expected), but the issue has never received much attention even from the social-democratic governments since 1990, despite their historic tradition of emphasizing such concerns. Social policies have focused more on reducing poverty (by providing targeted social benefits) and lately on managing social risk through social protection (see the next chapter) rather than on narrowing income gaps and reducing overall inequality.

Thus far, in the neoliberal period, economists have not been able to tell citizens what the lag time is between the implementation of an economic strategy that is supposed to create and spread the wealth by creating jobs (and thus also reduce poverty) and the remediation of broader social obstacles. As we demonstrated in Chapter 4, Chile has grown economically – but not for all – so any agenda for tackling the structural roots of inequality is already taking a backseat to macroeconomic and economic-growth policies by neoliberal default. The Concertación administrations continued to keep macroeconomic forces stabilized because they believed that doing so was fundamental to economic growth, but they were blinded by the dogma that economic growth would filter down to the lower echelons of society and that the social agenda could be focused on poverty reduction with only mild attention to the middle class and no real effort to reduce the economic power of the rich elites. This is what could be called the "neoliberal trap."

Annex: Taxation in Chile and in other OECD countries

Table A.1.

Tax Revenues as % of GDP, 2000–2008 Average

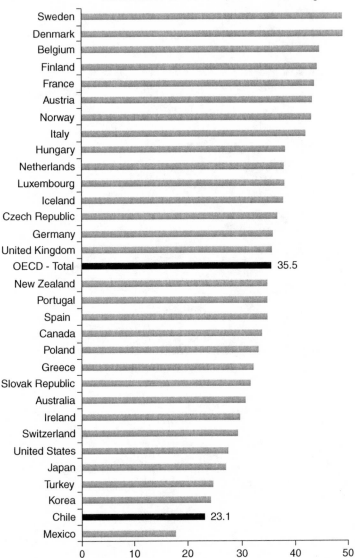

Table A.2. *Total Revenues and Tax Structure for Selected OECD Countries: Averages from 2000 to 2008*

Country	Total Tax Revenues (% GDP)	Tax Structure (% of Total Tax Revenues)				
		Personal Income Tax	Corporate Income Tax	Social Security Contributions	Taxes on Goods and Services (VAT)	Other Taxes
Chile	23.1	4.5	12.6	6.2	48.0	28.7
Czech Republic	36.8	12.3	12.1	43.6	30.6	1.4
France	43.7	17.5	6.6	36.9	25.2	13.8
Germany	35.8	24.9	4.4	39.1	28.9	2.7
Greece*	32.3	14.3	9.8	34.6	35.9	5.4
Hungary	38.1	18.8	6.1	30.9	38.9	5.3
Ireland	29.8	28.0	11.8	15.1	37.2	7.9
Italy	42.0	25.5	7.6	29.8	26.2	10.9
Japan*	27.0	18.9	14.4	37.0	19.4	10.3
Mexico	17.7	-	-	16.0	54.3	-
New Zealand	35.0	42.1	13.7	0.0	33.9	10.3
Poland*	33.1	13.2	6.8	38.2	37.3	4.5
Portugal	34.9	16.0	9.5	31.9	38.1	4.5
Spain	34.8	19.0	9.7	34.7	27.6	9.0
Turkey	24.5	17.4	7.1	21.7	46.4	7.4
United Kingdom	35.6	29.4	9.2	18.1	30.8	12.5
United States	27.6	37.6	9.3	24.6	17.2	11.3
OECD Total*	35.5	25.2	9.9	25.6	31.7	7.6

*Data until 2007
Source: OECD.

Table A.3. *Corporate, Personal, and VAT Tax Rates for Several OECD and Non-OECD Countries, Selected Years*

Country	Corporate Income Tax Rate (2010)	Corporate Income Tax Rate (2011)	Top Marginal Personal Income Tax Rates for Employee** (2009)	VAT(2010) (Range for Different State Rates)
Australia	30.0	30.0	46.5	10.0
Austria	25.0	25.0	42.7	20.0
Belgium	34.0	34.0	45.3	21.0
Canada*	29.4	27.6	46.4	5.0
Chile	19.0	19.0	40.0	19.0
Czech Republic	19.0	19.0	20.1	20.0
Denmark	25.0	25.0	54.8	25.0
Estonia	21.0	21.0	21.0	20.0
Finland	26.0	26.0	48.6	22.0
France	34.4	34.4	37.6	19.6
Germany*	30.2	30.2	47.5	19.0
Greece	24.0	20.0	33.6	19.0
Hungary	19.0	19.0	45.0	25.0
Iceland	18.0	20.0	35.7	25.5
Ireland	12.5	12.5	42.7	21.0
Israel*	25.0	24.0	45.0	16.0
Italy	27.5	27.5	40.2	20.0
Japan*	39.5	39.5	47.3	5.0
Korea*	24.2	24.2	35.4	10.0
Luxembourg*	28.6	28.8	34.7	15.0
Mexico	30.0	30.0	28.0	16.0
Netherlands	25.5	25.5	50.0	19.0
New Zealand	30.0	28.0	38.0	12.5
Norway	28.0	28.0	40.0	25.0
Poland	19.0	19.0	23.7	22.0
Portugal*	26.5	26.5	37.4	20.0
Slovak Republic	19.0	19.0	16.5	19.0
Slovenia	20.0	20.0	41.0	20.0
Spain	30.0	30.0	43.0	16.0
Sweden	26.3	26.3	56.5	25.0
Switzerland*	21.2	21.2	37.5	7.6
Turkey	20.0	20.0	35.6	18.0

(*continued*)

Table A.3. (*continued*)

Country	Corporate Income Tax Rate (2010)	Corporate Income Tax Rate (2011)	Top Marginal Personal Income Tax Rates for Employee** (2009)	VAT(2010) (Range for Different State Rates)
United Kingdom	28.0	26.0	40.0	17.5
United States*(1)	39.2	39.2	41.7	0–10.25
Latin America				
Argentina	35.0	35.0	35.0	21.0
Brazil	34.0	34.0	27.5	17–25
Colombia	33.0	33.0	33.0	16.0
Peru	30.0	30.0	30.0	18.0

* Taxes are combined for countries that have both national and federal taxes.
** Some of these are outdated owing to government reforms after the financial crisis of 2008–9.
(1) United States has no VAT; instead, it has a sales tax that varies from state to state.
Source: Own elaboration based on OECD tax database and Wikipedia.

6

The Social Policies of the 1990s and 2000s

Neoliberalism Tempered with Social Protection?

Introduction

After the return to democracy in 1990, the center-left coalition sought to redress the difficult social situation inherited from the Pinochet regime: poverty levels above 40 percent of the population, depressed real wages, and persistent unemployment and reduced social benefits. The new governments, while maintaining the basic pillars of the inherited economic model (opening to international trade, privatization, open capital mobility, and flexible labor markets), were more sensitive to the social conditions of the poor and wanted to reduce poverty, protect vulnerable groups, and, to the extent possible, spread the benefits of accelerated growth and prosperity more evenly across different groups. The main delusion of this strategy, however, was the belief that effective social progress could be accomplished without really tackling the root causes of high inequality and only by pursuing growth and targeted social policies.

In general, social policies evolve according to the broader development strategies adopted by governments. In practice, these policies are shaped by the concrete demands of different social groups for redistribution and social protection, by the amount of fiscal resources available to finance social policy, and by the political feasibility of pursuing certain social objectives. Under the development strategy of import substitution, in place from the 1930s to the 1970s in Chile, Latin America, and other developing countries, the main objectives of social policy were social modernization and the formation of human resources required by the industrialization process. The instruments for this were the expansion of education at various levels, including higher education (expansion of public universities) available at low cost or funded entirely by the state; housing policies able to address a growing urban population; national public health systems; and pay-as-go social security. Labor market policies involved legislation on minimum wages, severance payments, and restrictions on firings to ensure job stability of (incumbent) workers. Land reform was also implemented to correct a highly concentrated pattern of land tenure that characterized most Latin American countries. The social constituency behind these policies was composed of urban workers; labor unions in the public and private sectors; rural workers; and an ascendant middle class built around the urbanization process, the development of the state, and the expanding segment of small and middle-size enterprises. Social policies were geared to the interests of a broad coalition that included the (rural and urban) working class and the middle class.

The social policies of the past thirty years (with variations between the policies followed by the Pinochet regime and the subsequent center–left governments) were influenced by the principles set out by free-market economics and the Washington Consensus applied to the social sector and had the following common elements:

1. The target group of social policy was the "poor and vulnerable" more than the working class and the middle class. The poor could be a rural or an urban destitute person, a child, the elderly and the unemployed.
2. The main objective of social policy was poverty reduction rather than income distribution and lower wealth inequality. The dominant concept for measuring poverty was income.
3. The main means for social improvement was aggregate economic growth, which was to be stimulated by the triad of liberalization, stabilization, and privatization.
4. Privatization was encouraged in social services such as education, health care, and the provision of pensions. Private universities were subject to little regulation, and tuition and monthly fees paid by the students rose significantly. A model prevailed in which private universities perhaps resembled more a "factory of professionals" than learning institutions that combined teaching with research and external dissemination. In turn, primary and secondary schools and health-services delivery were seen as business activities.

5. Social security was privatized, and mandatory enrolment in the AFP system prevailed.

These market-oriented social policies are very controversial. Their conceptual design entails at least five important considerations: (1) The lack of an adequate consideration of issues of social and economic rights. In fact, the logic of social rights (to free or low-cost education, health, decent retirement) is replaced by a market logic in which the purchasing power of the beneficiary is the main driving force in access to these social services. (2) Neglecting inequality of income and wealth as an explicit and valid focus of social policy. (3) Focusing on targeting the very poor at the cost of neglecting the middle class as a valid subject of social policy. (4) An underestimation of issues of asymmetric information, quality control, and regulation in the private delivery of complex social services. (5) Neglecting issues of social participation, governance, and economic democracy.

Table 6.1 presents a "social matrix" that shows the content and main (qualitative) results of the social and other public policies undertaken by the Aylwin, Frei, Lagos, and Bachelet governments in areas such as poverty reduction, inequality, focalization of public spending, and minimum wages.

As shown in Table 6.1, the outlook is one of certain advances and progress in some areas, such as poverty reduction (subject to the qualifications expressed in Chapter 5), the creation of unemployment insurance, expansion of the beneficiaries of the public health system through the AUGE plan (the Spanish acronym for Universal Access with Explicit Guarantees), and reforms in social security. As we shall discuss later, however, the reach and impact of these policies were often hampered by various factors: the self-imposed strictures and conceptual straitjackets of refusing to depart, in a significant way, from the orthodoxies of the market-oriented social policies highlighted above; the power of the lobbies for profit-oriented private providers of education, health services, and pension-fund managing companies that would be affected by a more aggressive and comprehensive expansion of the role of the state in social sectors; and the overall constraint of resources to conduct social policy demanded by a moderate level of overall tax collection by the state (see Table A.1 in the Annex of Chapter 5).

Table 6.1. *Social Matrix by Government Administration, 1990–2009*

	Aylwin Administration (1990–1994)	Frei Administration (1994–1999)	Lagos Administration (2000–2005)	Bachelet Administration (2006–2009)
Official Poverty	Decreases	Decreases	Decreases	Decreases
Inequality (Gini Coefficient*)	High	High	High	Marginal decrease
Increase and Focalization of Subsidies	Yes	Yes	Yes	Yes
Minimum Wage	Real Increase	Real Increase	Real Increase	Real Increase
Education:				
- Expenditures	Increase	Increase	Increase	Increase
- Reforms	Program P-900 (poor schools), program MECE (quality of education)	School day extension, teacher evaluation	Compulsory 12 years of education, digital alphabetization	Educational reform (LGE), subsidies for preferential education
Health:				
- Expenditures	Increase	Increase	Increase	Increase
- Reforms	Strengthening of public hospitals, coverage extension	Strengthening of public hospitals, coverage extension	AUGE plan, modification in law regarding ISAPRES	Crece Contigo program (child-protection policies)

Social Security Reforms	No	No	No	Pension reform, "universal" basic pension
Explicit Goals of Lower-Income Inequality	No	No	No	No
Limits to Concentration of Property	No	No	No	Partial
Strengthening of Trade Unions and Social Organizations	Light	Light	Light	Light
Consumer Protection	Light	Light	Creation of a board of free competition, modification of consumer law	More active
Democratization in the Access to Credit	Partial	Partial	Partial / Increases	Partial / Increases
Unemployment Insurance	No	No	Unemployment insurance for formal private-sector workers	Modifications in coverage

Source: Own elaboration and Solimano and Pollack (2006).

97

The Social Policies of the 1990s

During the 1990s, Christian-Democrat presidents Patricio Aylwin and Eduardo Frei Ruiz-Tagle started to deal with the urgent social deficits inherited from the military period. Resource constraints in social sectors were eased (through tax increases in addition to revenues coming from economic growth). Public spending in social areas increased. The real value of the minimum wage was restored and increased. There were also important increases in monetary subsidies to the poor, together with more funds to chronically underfunded public health services, education, housing, and pensions. To finance the social programs, the Aylwin government increased, in agreement with the right-wing opposition, corporate income tax from 10 percent (set in 1988) to 15 percent in 1990. An effort was made to avoid curbing social expenditures at times of fiscal imbalances (an expedient used several times during the military regime).

During the Aylwin administration, a ministry of social planning was created (known as MIDEPLAN).[1] In turn, there was a revamping of such public infrastructure as roads, highways, and ports that had deteriorated after years of public investment neglect. Further, an environmental regulatory entity was created to promote sustainable development and assess the environmental impact of major investment projects, the CONAMA (Corporación Nacional del Medio Ambiente).

The Frei administration[2] tried to enhance the level and quality of education through the improvement of the physical infrastructure of the school system, introduced changes in the school curriculum, and extended the length of time students spent in school. Moreover, an effort was made to improve the depressed levels of salaries of

---

[1] This actually corresponded to a status elevation of the existent ODEPLAN (*Oficina de Planificacion Nacional*, National Planning Office), created in the late 1960s. In the 1970s and 1980s, ODEPLAN played an important role in devising free-market reforms in education and health care, as well as antipoverty programs, during the Pinochet regime.

[2] President Frei emphasized further integration into the world economy and signed free-trade agreements with several countries, such as Canada and Mexico, and became a member of APEC, WTO, and MERCOSUR. This trend was later continued by President Ricardo Lagos and a free trade agreement with the United States, the EU, and China.

schoolteachers, raise benefits, and strengthen job protection under the Teachers Statute (Estatuto Docente) approved in the early 1990s. Other actions taken by the new democratic governments were directed at reducing the housing deficit. During the 1990s, approximately 800,000 new houses were built, twice as much as in the 1980s.

The Social Policies of the 2000s

Although the overall spirit of the economic and social policies of the two socialist presidents, Lagos and Bachelet, was one of continuity with the economic policies of the 1990s (and were even more orthodox in macroeconomic policy, as discussed in Chapter 4), there was a change in emphasis toward policies of social protection – pensions, unemployment benefits, preschools, health services, and others. The Bachelet administration employed the rhetoric of a state of social rights in which ensuring benefits to the population by law would shield them from the vagaries of the political and economic cycles. (This rationale, to an extent, also informed Lagos's reform in the health sector through the AUGE plan.)

We shall focus on the following policies of the 2000s:

(a) the Chile Solidario antipoverty program,
(b) reforms in education,
(c) reforms in the health sector (the AUGE plan),
(d) the pension reform of 2008, and
(e) labor legislation and unemployment insurance.

Antipoverty Efforts

One reformed antipoverty program launched in the Lagos administration is Chile Solidario.[3] This program was aimed at very poor households through the improvement of targeting and performance of already existing social benefits for low-income families and entailed a more comprehensive approach to poverty that went beyond the

---

[3] A complete reference (albeit in a self-congratulatory vein) of the social reforms and policies of the 2000s in Chile is found in Larrañaga and Contreras (2010).

income dimension.[4] The total transfers embodied in Chile-Solidario amounted to US$100 per month per participating family in 2005, or close to one-third of the average income of poor households (CASEN 2006). As of mid-2008, close to 310,000 households had enrolled in the program, and nearly 40 percent of beneficiary households were headed by women. The program was strongly targeted at the very poor (according to Larrañaga et al. (2010), about 99 percent of the beneficiaries were from the lowest ventile in 2008). This entailed a higher degree of targeting than similar programs in other Latin American countries, such as Oportunidades in Mexico and Bolsa Familia in Brazil.[5]

Reforms in Education

The democratic governments since 1990 were reluctant to open political debate on changing the LOCE (Ley Orgánica Constitucional de Educación, Organic Constitutional Law of Education), which came from the military regime. They wanted to avoid clashing with conservative forces close to the former military regime and sympathetic to the prevailing education system. The LOCE assigned municipalities the mandate to manage schools and appoint school directors in the public and subsidized systems; in turn, this constitutional law granted very liberal conditions to set up private universities (almost unregulated) and severely constrained public funding for state universities: as of 2010, it is estimated that the direct contribution of the state to public universities in Chile is, on average, less than 20 percent. In fact, according to a joint OECD–World Bank report on higher education, approximately 80 percent of the university cost is borne by student fees and other charges. Surprisingly

---

[4] Chile Solidario operated on the basis of a direct link between the beneficiary family and a professional of the program who works personally with the beneficiary family for about two years until "graduation." Exiting the program required compliance with some fifty-three minimum conditions.

[5] The Lagos administration raised the VAT from 18 percent to 19 percent in 2003. There was also an increase in the corporate income tax rate, from 15 percent to 17 percent, a tax rate well below those of other Latin American countries. Incidentally, the Piñera administration in 2010 increased corporate income taxes to 19 percent to help finance reconstruction in the wake of the earthquake of February 27, 2010 (see Annex in Chapter 5).

for a developing country, the share of the budget of Chilean families devoted to paying for university fees and tuition is *three to four times* higher than in Europe.[6]

The main university student unions – FECH (Federación de Estudiantes de Chile), FEUC (Federación de Estudiantes de la Pontificia Universidad Católica de Chile), the Student Federation of Universidad de Santiago de Chile, and others – as well as the Colegio de Profesores de Chile, the teachers union for the primary and secondary school system, and later the rectors of state universities were in general quite critical of the Concertación governments' "politics of consensus and pragmatism" in education that sanctioned an expensive, segmented, and unequal system at different levels. The student movement evinced a specific contempt for the lack of enforcement of the law that dictated that private universities were to be not-for-profit entities. Nevertheless, owners of private universities managed to get profit distribution through parallel companies that rent building space and other assets to universities. Another highly contentious issue has been the retreat of state funding to public universities, shifting the cost of higher education to families. This criticism reached high points in 2006 and above all in 2011.[7]

The education system in Chile is strongly pro–private sector. The number of private schools receiving a state subsidy by means of a voucher scheme has been growing since the early 2000s, whereas the number of public schools receiving it has been declining.[8] A similar trend is evident in the sharp decline in enrollment in public schools (see Figure 6.1, panels A and B). Its consequences for social equality and upward mobility remain to be seen in a highly unequal society such as Chile's. The most likely outcome is for the education system to reproduce and exacerbate current inequality.

[6] See *Reviews of National Policies for Education: Tertiary Education in Chile* (OECD-World Bank, 2009).

[7] The Concertación policies were to increase resources for public schools, raise the salary of teachers (severely deteriorated during the military period), and invest in the physical renovation and construction of schools. This increase in resources, however, was unable to contain the growing gap between private and public schools in the quality of education.

[8] The Lagos administration extended mandatory education to twelve years in order to get a job, hence fostering education completion among students.

Panel A

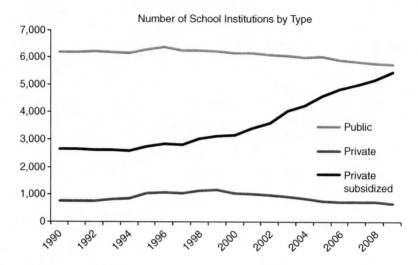

Panel B

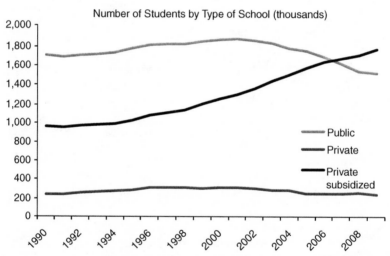

Figure 6.1 Chile – Evolution of public, private, and private subsidized schools
(panel A) and school enrollment (panel B), 1990–2009.
Source: Chilean Ministry of Education.

Box 6.1 The Dramatic Shifts of Chilean Education in the 1970s and 1980s

In the late 1960s, the government of President Eduardo Frei Montalva had practically universalized primary education by introducing double shifts and establishing an eight-year basic education cycle. It simultaneously expanded secondary and higher education, modernized the curriculum, and improved teacher training. At the beginning of the 1970s, the government of Salvador Allende sought to broaden educational opportunities to workers and marginalized groups. Later on, it launched curricular and institutional reforms more aligned with his social and economic transformation program of socialist orientation, called the ENU (Escuela Nacional Unificada, National Unified School System). These reforms were opposed by part of the church and the political opposition of the time, and the government was not able to implement these reforms before being overthrown by the military coup of September 11, 1973. The flair for expansion and democratization of education also reached the universities under the movement of *Universidad para Todos* (University for All).

The end of the Allende government and its replacement by a military regime led to a dramatic reversal in these trends toward democratization of education. The chief goal of the military regime was the introduction of a private-sector-oriented education system. In 1980, the military government launched a profound market-based education reform, again to put it in line with its overall free-market revolution. Its objective was to promote greater private-sector participation in delivering education services at all levels and to support the creation of an unregulated system of private universities, an endeavor that proved to be highly profitable for the owners of private universities; the quality of education and the lack of research activities is another matter. But the military regime was all too aware of the role of the education system in transmitting ideology and values to future generations and the potential of student mobilizations for progressive social change. Consequently, on its last day in office in early 1990, the military junta, exploiting its legislative primacy, passed the LOCE before a newly elected parliament could be installed. The law made it difficult to amend the education reforms of 1980 and 1981, as one of its provisions required that any constitutional change made by a new parliament be passed by a qualified majority. Thus, despite the change in political administration in 1990, the military regime's educational administrative and organizational structure remained in place, negating momentum for reforms in this critical sector of Chile's society.The new system established by the LOCE ceded responsibility for operating public schools to the municipalities, a duty previously under the general management of the Ministry of Education. Resources were allotted on a per capita basis, and the system was supposed to foster open competition between publicly and privately administered schools. Government subsidies were provided to private and public schools for each student enrolled, creating a voucher system for grade levels K–12, covering a student's entire school cycle. The "municipalization" of kindergarten, primary, and secondary schools was complete by 1986. The effect of this law was that national subsidies, or the voucher system, divided the Chilean system into three types of schools: municipal or public schools, private subsidized schools (*escuelas municipales subvencionadas*), and privately paid schools. Currently, the ratio of per-student resources is approximately one to six between public (municipal) schools and all private schools. The highly segmented education system replicates well-entrenched inequalities in society, in step with a sociopolitical model aimed at reconstituting the consciousness of a country in conformance with capitalist development.

Despite the reluctance of the center-left governments to overhaul the institutional framework in the education sector inherited from the military regime, President Bachelet was forced to start a process to change the LOCE as a response to increasing activism, in the fall and winter of 2006, by the secondary-school student movement, which demanded radical reform in a more egalitarian direction. A main demand of the students, that has been consistent over time, is the end of the dominant role of the profit motive in the management of the education system in Chile.

After proper dilution, neutralization, and delaying of the main democratic demands of the spontaneous student movement, the Bachelet government crafted a consensus with the political establishment and, in haste, proposed legislation to replace the LOCE. Notice that even though the law passed the parliament, it was not accepted by most of the reforming movement (the new law was less "reformist" than originally proposed owing to political negotiations with the right-wing

---

Box 6.2 The Secondary Student ("Penguin") Revolution of 2006

On April 24, 2006, an important social movement emerged, highly critical of the prevailing education system inherited from the Pinochet regime and maintained in place by the subsequent governments. The movement was termed the "Penguin Revolution" because of the Penguin-like uniform of school students. The movement began as a reaction against school bus fares and university entrance fees but evolved into a national movement demanding "quality education for all." From April to June 2006, student leaders orchestrated a series of demonstrations, strikes, and school takeovers, and support for public school students grew, attracting the participation of university students, teachers, and parents as well as private-school students. The movement peaked with a national strike on May 30, in which several hundred thousand demonstrating secondary students, along with many university students, paralyzed almost all Chile's schools and universities. When police exerted excessive force against the student protesters, an outraged public pressured President Bachelet to become directly involved in negotiations with the student leaders. Following a second national strike, the government announced several new measures that met some of the students' demands. Officially, the strike ended on June 12, although smaller-scale demonstrations and takeovers continued across the country.

---

opposition). The new LGE (Ley General de Eduación) sought improvement of the "quality" of education, the strengthening of regulation for mixed (subsidized) schools, new government entities, less flexibility for schools in selecting students (to protect against discrimination), among other reforms. Yet it was apparent that these reforms did not address some critical demands by students, teachers, and the education community, because the final law did not change what they saw as the central problems of the educational system: schools as for-profit organizations, the subsidy system, and public schools' dependence on municipalities. Also, the new reforms have done little to reduce the big gap in per-student resources between the private and public school systems, which tends to perpetuate the already unequal income and wealth distribution.

The LGE also fostered a new education quality-assurance system, with two agencies responsible for school supervision and accountability: the Education Quality Agency (Agencia de Calidad) and the Superintendent of Education. In addition, the Bachelet administration also introduced a separate bill to modify the institutional framework of publicly managed education and provide additional funding and technical pedagogical support to public schools. A "preferential subsidy" was introduced in 2008 that provided public schools with an extra subsidy per student belonging to the 40 percent lower income families of the country. This subsidy covers preschooling and the entirety of the primary-school years and amounts to a nearly 50 percent increase in actual benefits.[9]

Box 6.3 The Chilean University System

Until 1980, higher education in Chile consisted of a comparatively simple and consolidated system. There were two main public universities, Universidad de Chile and Universidad Católica de Chile, followed by Universidad de Santiago (until 1973, the Universidad Técnica del Estado). These universities had campuses in most provinces in the country but after the military coup were forced to operate only in Santiago in an effort to break down national universities. Public universities were created by law and funded in part by the government, which provided about 65 percent of their total budget. Under the military regime, the system underwent a total transformation, including funding arrangements. The provincial branches of public universities were turned into autonomous, regional public institutions, and their names changed. This was intended to curtail the social and political influence of the older public universities, and new legislation made it possible to establish private higher-education institutions provided that one of the previously existing universities (either among the original eight or any of the new public regional ones) agreed to examine students and thus supervise the quality of teaching. State funding to public universities was greatly reduced, and institutions were asked to find new sources

---

[9] Another program aimed at the education sector is the *Chile Crece Contigo*, based on the diagnosis that psychosocial development gaps already exist at the beginning of formal education and tend to be reproduced later in the rest of the formation cycle. This program seeks equalization of "starting conditions" for children 0 to 4 (preschool years). The initiative fosters care and development of children in poorer families, provided the beneficiaries belong to other social programs.

of income. University tuition and fees rose sharply. The system was further diversified into three institutional tiers – universities, which granted professional and academic degrees; professional institutes, which could offer professional but not academic degrees; and technical training centers, offering two-year technical degrees.

Since 1980, the system has grown significantly. In 2009, there were sixty-one universities (thirty-six of them private), forty-five professional institutes, and seventy-four technical training centers. Nevertheless, there are signs that the system is increasingly being consolidated and regrouped, as some of the larger private universities are acquiring control of other institutions in a sort of market for universities.

In addition, the budget devoted by Chilean families to pay for public universities is probably among the highest in the world – 28 percent of household income per capita, whereas in the United States and the United Kingdom, this is 11 percent and 5 percent, respectively. For private universities, the budget spend by households is among the highest too, after the United States (OECD-WB, 2009). Private universities in Chile are strongly oriented toward teaching. Research is, generally, a low priority and almost nonexistent in many private universities, although a few of them are beginning to foster some research activities. The new system has expanded sharply the enrollment in the university system to around one million students, but dropout rates, mainly among low-income students, are significant.

Health Sector

A main reform of the 2000s in the health sector was the Lagos government's AUGE plan, which sent various proposed health-system reforms to parliament between 2003 and 2005, dealing with both the regulatory side of the ISAPRES system (which had been under scrutiny during its twenty-five years) and the coverage side of the entire system. The public AUGE system provides a set of legally mandated guarantees for health-service coverage, based on a prioritized list of diagnoses and treatments for fifty-six health conditions. Another reform was the creation of an independent Superintendent of Health, an agency that now tries to ensure standards for the quality of care by and guidelines for the financial operations of the ISAPRES insurers.

These reforms tried to address some of the most visible problems affecting the Chilean health systems ISAPRES and FONASA (the National Health Fund, the public tier of the system): high inequality in access to health services and segmentation according to the income levels of the beneficiary, long waiting lists, limited focus on prevention, and high costs and financial uncertainties in covering very high-cost disease treatments.[10] The AUGE plan sought to ensure the basic right of access to health services for any Chilean (the explicit guarantee component). By law (although not necessarily in practice, given waiting periods and hospital availability), the most relevant and recurrent diseases are to be attended on time, either by the public or the private system (in case the service could not be provided in the public sector), under specific quality standards (only by accredited institutions and certified doctors), with a pre-fixed monetary charge calculated according to income that must not exceed 20 percent of total costs. The coverage includes individuals enrolled in the public and private systems and those not enrolled in any health system. Guarantees are ensured for more than fifty specified diseases that account for nearly two-thirds of conditions recorded in the population.[11]

Box 6.4 The Chilean Health System – A Comparatively Sophisticated System that Favors the More Healthy and Prosperous

In 1952, Chile became one of the first Latin American nations to establish a comprehensive national public-health system, providing all citizens equal access to health services, regardless of the level of income of the beneficiary and extending to both urban and rural

---

[10] The two main criticisms of Chile's dual public-private system have been that (1) those enrolled in the private insurance system of ISAPRES have access to higher-quality secondary and tertiary care beyond the primary care provided under the public health system (they can receive more specialized, refined care for certain conditions), and (2) the ISAPRES insurers can self-select their participants – excluding high-risk patients or patients with prior or existing conditions – thus funneling more expensive patients back into the public system. (On top of that, employers who are able to offer these ISAPRES plans to their employees also receive a tax break from the government.)

[11] A key element of this reform is that when public supply is not sufficient to provide access on time to the beneficiary, the private sector will take care of that patient, and the cost will be borne by the public sector. In principle, this implies incentives for the public sector to improve efficiency and allocation in order to avoid the high costs of the private sector.

areas. Called the National Health Service (Servicio Nacional de Salud), the new initiative achieved important reductions in infant mortality, contagious disease, and chronic illness. The system led to an improvement of several health indicators of the population, a sharp reduction in infant mortality and malnutrition, in addition to a cut in disease incidence and contagion.

The system remained in place until 1979, when the Pinochet regime reformed the health system by calling for increased private-sector participation. In 1980, all primary health-care services – including their management and the facilities at which they are provided – devolved to the local municipalities (340 municipal governments at that time). As such, the proportion of GDP spent by the government on public health fell sharply during the military regime. After 1990, the new democratic governments increased health expenditures, and more resources were devoted to public hospitals.

The system created by the Pinochet regime is still in place today. It consists of a public and private health-care structures. The public component is called the National Health Fund (FONASA), which is open to anyone; it is funded from general state revenues and a contribution of 7 percent from the taxable income of those who are employed. For those unable to afford services (whether because they are unemployed and/or come from low-income or indigent segments of the population), health care is free – funded not only from general revenues but also the contributions of higher-income individuals who use the system. As of December 2009, it serves approximately three-quarters of the population.

The second, private component was implemented in 1981 as a system of privately run providers of health services (ISAPRES) that serve as both health insurers and service providers. This new market for health care is one in which the purchasing power of beneficiaries is the main determinant of the amount and quality of health services for the population. Participants in ISAPRES instruct their employers to put a payroll health deduction into an account with one of these insurer providers, with the amount depending on the type of insurance policy they select, although always with a 7 percent floor. ISAPRES benefited around 16 percent of total population by end of 2009.

There are alternatives to these two systems, including special health systems for the military, police, and general armed forces. Furthermore, there are people – particularly the very wealthy – who do not belong to any system and who have access to private-care hospitals and services that are not part of the universal health-care system.

Figure 6.2, panel A, shows that the bulk of the population (73.5 percent as of December 2009) is served in the public system and that this trend was increasing during the 2000s following escalating fees charged by ISAPRES. For many middle-class families, let alone the poor, the private ISAPRES system is close to unaffordable. Its orientation to higher levels of income is shown in panel B of Figure 6.2, which shows that ISAPRES's affiliation goes up sharply for individuals with monthly income above US$1,800.

The AUGE plan was not accompanied by serious reform (i.e., regulatory and otherwise) of the ISAPRES system oriented toward reducing the fees paid by the beneficiaries and increasing the coverage provided by this system to lower-income individuals beyond what is strictly profitable for the private providers (although now beneficiaries enrolled in AUGE can receive services rendered by ISAPRES and paid for by the state if the public system is unable to provide the health services entitled by the AUGE system). In turn, the costs of the creation and operation of the AUGE are not borne by wealthier people (through higher personal income or corporate taxation, for example). In fact, the reform was financed by a rise in VAT, which is not a progressive tax.

An evaluation of the full benefits and impact of the AUGE plan is still pending.[12] On the positive side, there is evidence that access to evaluation and treatment of diseases such as cancer and cardiac afflictions has increased with improvements in early detection resulting in lower mortality. In addition, the costs of treatments for the beneficiary have declined (lower co-payment and financial protection in case of high costs). The system operates, however, by implicit rationing and with somewhat significant waiting times for patients seeking attention in public hospitals. Moreover, the costs of prescriptions and drugs remain high.

Pension Reforms

Another policy of social protection was the pension reform undertaken by President Bachelet.[13] After twenty-five years of operation, it became

---

[12] A useful description of the AUGE plan in terms of design, application, results, and pending problems is found in Infante and Paraje (2010).

[13] In 1924, Chile became the first country in the Western Hemisphere to introduce a state-run pension system when it established a retirement fund for manual laborers. That fund was the predecessor of the Servicio de Seguro Social (the Social Security Service), established in 1952, which was to become the main retirement system for the majority of Chilean workers until 1981. This was a pay-as-you-go system in which

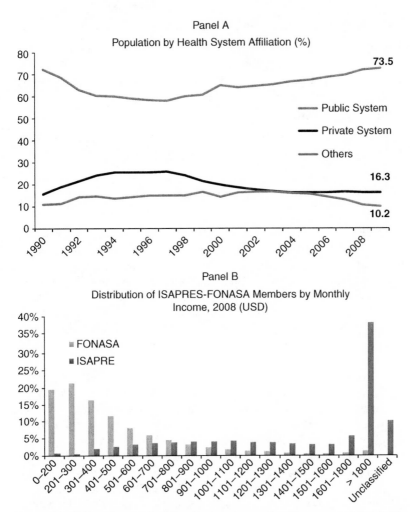

Figure 6.2 Chile – Population distribution among health systems, 1990–2009 period (panel A), and distribution of population among health systems depending on income level, 2008 (panel B).

Source: Own elaboration based on data from health superintendence.

the benefits of retirees were paid from the contributions of active workers. In addition, special-interest legislation led to the creation of more than 100 different pension schemes with widely different benefits that were tied neither to the level of contributions nor to different retirement ages for different groups of workers. In 1978, the military government reformed the pay-as-you-go system by standardizing retirement at age 65 for men and age 60 for women, eliminating special regimens, and rationalizing indexing, all of which preceded the implementation of its new capitalization system in 1981. The armed forces were left outside the private capitalization system.

apparent that the private capitalization pension (AFP) system was able to deliver pensions only for workers with stable jobs, high wages, and a culture of making permanent contributions to the system. In the privatized system, a worker needed twenty years of continuous contributions to be eligible to receive a minimum pension. As many people often changed jobs during their working life and sometimes could not afford (or just neglected) to make contributions between jobs, a comparatively low share of workers was eligible for minimum pension.

Box 6.5 The Privatization of Social Security in the Early 1980s (the Private Capitalization System)

On November 4, 1980, the military government, under its legislative primacy (as no elected parliament was in place at that time), passed a law that established a new private pension system in which private administration companies (Administradoras de Fondos de Pensiones, AFPs) offered individual pension accounts and managed the investment of those funds. The state was barred from managing the pension accounts, and no state-owned AFP was allowed (a feature that remains in place today). The private capitalization system remains mandatory for all dependent workers who entered the labor force after January 1, 1983, and optional for self-employed workers, just like the government system was. Workers already in the labor force before January 1983 had the option of staying in the old, government-run system or moving to the new system. Workers who moved to the newly privatized pension system received recognition bonds from the government, which acknowledged the contributions they had already made to the old system; those who stayed in the old pension system (the Instituto de Normalización Previsional, INP, later turned into the Instituto de Prevision Social, IPS) had their pension rights guaranteed.

Each AFP operates the equivalent of a mutual fund that invests in stocks, bonds, and government debt. The AFP is administratively separate from the mutual fund, so if the AFP goes bankrupt, the assets of the mutual fund – that is, workers' investments – would, in principle, be unaffected. Workers are free to change from one AFP to another, although in practice there are few transfers among management funds. The AFP management companies charge a fee for managing the funds, and estimates are that their average rate of return on their business can be greater than 40 percent. The Superintendent of AFP is the regulatory body that oversees AFP activities.

In March 2008, the Bachelet government enacted a law to ensure a "system of solidarity pensions," which entailed a basic solidarity pension and an additional pension contribution. Every Chilean over the age of 65 is eligible for the basic solidarity pension. In line with the philosophy of targeting and conditional benefits, the solidarity pension is available to the poorer 60 percent of the population not receiving a pension through the private system and who have resided in Chile for at least twenty years. The basic pension was set at $75,000, or roughly US$150 per month, and represented a substantial increase over previous pension payments for low-income people.[14] The additional pension contribution, in turn, is a monetary transfer to beneficiaries with low contributions and who belong to targeted socioeconomic groups that satisfy the residence criteria.

The new law also introduced elements of gender equality among the beneficiaries and encouraged the participation of independent workers, self-employed individuals, and small entrepreneurs in the AFP system. This brought new contingents that started to be covered by the private capitalization system, forcing them to contribute to AFP. For the pension fund managing companies, this expanded the number of clients and augmented the range of profitable operations. Summing up, the new system is based on three pillars: (1) a solidarity pillar (*pilar solidario*), whereby workers can contribute to two benefits: a basic pension (*pensión básica solidaria*) and a contributory pension (*aporte solidario*) consisting of a bonus contribution to supplement the lowest-accumulating pensions (above a certain threshold, the individual may make only a minimum bonus contribution); (2) a voluntary pillar (*pilar voluntario*), whose purpose is to facilitate and encourage nonobligatory savings for old age for people with limited savings capacities; and (3) a sole contributory pillar (*pilar contributivo*), consisting of individual capitalization contributions, to which some changes have been made to improve the degree of competition among AFPs and the transparency of the private system.

The degree of "private sector friendliness" (read the power of the lobby of the AFP) of the last pension reform just described is

---

[14] Previous to the reforms were basic pensions for retired and disabled people, whose benefits were increased an equivalent of 40–50 percent and extended to segments of the population previously not eligible.

demonstrated by the fact that the reform of the pensions system was unable to grant the Chilean state the possibility of running its own public pension-management company, one that could compete with the private AFPs; thus, the system of AFPs consolidated its virtual monopoly on the private capitalization pension system, managing at a considerable profit the pension funds of more than 4 million people in Chile who have no real voice and participation in the investments of their savings for old age beyond changing from one fund to another according to its risk-return profile. In turn, the sector has been concentrating over time. As of 2011, only six private AFPs were in the market, down from twenty-two AFPs in 1996 (and up from five in 2008). It is apparent that the AFP consortium is an active lobby with strong political influence and wields a remarkable capacity for blocking any substantial reform that could threaten its protected niche in the pension business.

Labor Legislation and Unemployment Insurance

Chile's labor market is characterized by job fragility – frequent shifts of workers across jobs and from employment to unemployment, as well as a low level of unionization (Riesco 2008).[15] This job fragility and vulnerability is particularly serious for women and low-skilled workers. The labor market is also highly segmented between the formal and informal sectors.[16] Working conditions are generally worse in the informal sector (longer working hours and unsafe workplaces). Moreover, large firms in the formal sector have higher capital ratios, better technologies, and pay higher wage rates than small and medium-size enterprises, many of them in the informal sector. According to Infante (2011), the informal economy accounts for nearly 40 percent of total employment in the Chilean economy. In turn, informality of employment affects more women (43.4 percent) than men (37 percent), and informality is more acute in micro, small, and medium-size firms

---

[15] The link between the social conditions of Chile's population and how its labor market operates has been studied by Riesco (2008), Solimano and Pollack (2007), and Infante and Sunkel (2004).

[16] Formal sector jobs often (but not always) entail a job contract, social security, and health and other social benefits. Informal sector jobs, in turn, may have no job contracts and lack social security protection and benefits.

than in large companies. According to this study, income per worker in the formal sector is 36.5 percent higher than in the informal sector.

The pension reform of 2008 tried to increase coverage of pensions to self-employed workers. Unemployment insurance, however, covers only workers employed in the formal sector.

The legal framework ruling labor-capital relations was not subject to significant reforms under the socialist presidents Lagos and Bachelet during the 2000s. These reforms are a long-held aspiration of the labor movement and were intended to rebalance the skewed power relations between capital and labor in Chile. In the early 1990s, the new Aylwin administration reformed some aspects of Pinochet's labor code, repealing the most severe restrictions on trade unions (union leaders stopped being routinely incarcerated for labor activism); nevertheless, collective bargaining is banned at the industry level and has to be conducted at the level of individual firms. The current labor code still makes it difficult for trade unions to organize in many sectors. Unions are banned for public sector employees, and many employees in other sectors are still covered by individual contracts that stipulate that employees may not participate in collective bargaining. Both socialist presidents Lagos and Bachelet maintained the legal restrictions on interindustry collective bargaining and on collective bargaining in the public sector. The Central Unitaria de Trabajadores, CUT, a large labor confederation that was strong during the Allende government and before, has proposed new labor-law reforms to improve union rights and to give more power to unions, but its proposal has not been brought before parliament for discussion.

Unemployment Insurance

To reduce the social impact of labor layoffs, an unemployment-insurance mechanism was introduced in 2002 and modified again in 2009 to extend its coverage.[17] As already mentioned, the new insurance covers workers employed with contracts in the formal private sector, and it is not available to self-employed workers, people in the informal sector, and the employees in the public sector (half of whom work with temporary one-year contracts). The unemployment insurance was

---

[17] See Ramos and Acero (2010).

intended to complement severance payments, and its financial operation entails a (mandatory) personal savings account and a smaller Solidarity Unemployment Fund, which enables the worker to receive a payment independent of his or her contribution. The first fund is financed by the employer and, in case of undefined contract length, by the worker too. From 2003 to 2008, approximately 75 percent of beneficiaries have been workers under a fixed-term contract who have received an average benefit of 41 percent of their wages.[18] In the economic crisis of 2009, when unemployment in Chile was greater than 11percent of the workforce, insurance benefits reached almost 180,000 beneficiaries (in June), but the number of unemployed owing to the recession climbed to near 1 million people. This showed the limited coverage of the unemployment insurance scheme.[19]

Levels of Unionization

The extent to which workers are unionized in Chile is one measure of how far the effective enjoyment of labor rights has fallen in recent decades. The degree of unionization started to decline during the military regime, and the trend has continued in the new democracy. Before the 1973 military coup, the rate of unionization was more than 20 percent; by 1990, it had declined to 16 percent, and by 2009 to below 15 percent. In addition, the coverage of collective bargaining for total workers is even lower, reaching approximately 9 percent by 2006 (Riesco 2008).

The degree of labor union affiliation in Chile can be put in international perspective. As shown in Table 6.2, union density is low with respect to most European countries but higher than in the United States, France, and Turkey.

---

[18] The rest of the beneficiaries correspond to undefined-length contract workers. Those using only their individual accounts received 50 percent of their previous wages, while those using the Solidarity Fund as well received around 86 percent of their previous wages.

[19] Unemployment insurance was reformed in 2009, mainly introducing more protection, higher benefits, and added flexibility to funds administration in order to promote profitability of funds, etc. There are still many issues pending to improve the system, such as how to protect around 40% of workers who work independently or in the informal sector, differentiate according to size of family group, among others.

Table 6.2. *Labor Union Density in Chile and Selected Countries (Percentage)*

Country	Density (2008)
Australia	18.6
Canada	27.1
Chile	13.9
Czech Republic	20.2
Denmark	67.6
Finland	67.5
France	7.7
Germany	19.1
Ireland	32.3
Japan	18.2
Mexico[1]	17.4
Poland	15.6
Portugal	20.4
Spain	14.3
Sweden	68.3
Turkey	5.8
United States	11.9

[1] Data for 2005.
Source: OECD.

Box 6.6 A Stringent Labor Code Was First Introduced under Pinochet, and Little Progress Has Been Made Since

After the military coup of September 1973, the authorities followed a highly repressive stance toward labor unions in an attempt to break the backbone of a social movement that was a main source of support of the Allende government. To reduce the explosive inflation rate of 1973, the military government actively applied policies in which wage adjustments were delayed behind inflation. These policies led, as could be expected, to a severe drop in real wages. By mid-1979, the government adopted a policy of 100 percent wage indexation and also decided to legalize collective bargaining and eliminate a series of de facto restrictions imposed on labor bargaining.

However, in 1981, union membership and collective bargaining were heavily restricted. The labor reform code of 1981, designed by Jose Piñera Echeñique (labor minister and an older brother of President Sebastian Piñera Echeñique), restricted collective bargaining negotiations at the firm level. Unions and collective bargaining were viewed with distrust, in the neoliberal vein, mostly as interference in the normal adjustment of markets. The economic view of decentralized and atomistic labor markets made a good marriage with the political goal of the military regime to weaken a labor movement that might offer resistance to policies of privatization and the dominance of employers in labor relations and business in general. The right to strike was recognized but limited in its scope.

Under the Pinochet Labor Code, a union could be formed within a company with the consent of at least eight workers, if that number represented 50 percent of the total number of workers in the company. In larger companies, the process required the consent of 200 workers, regardless of whether those 200 were equivalent to 50 percent of the total number of workers in that company. The Labor Code permitted union membership only within a company. Collective bargaining for wage increases, better social benefits, and safer working conditions was not allowed at the level of industrial branches and could not be conducted by a federation or confederation of unions representing workers from the same productive sector.

Concluding Remarks

The post-Pinochet governments aimed at reducing poverty and the incidence of social risks without altering labor relations or the for-profit provision of social services. The tools were increased social expenditure, higher minimum wages, the gradual strengthening of institutions managing social policy, and expanded physical infrastructure. In the 2000s, social policy emphasized social protection and social rights. Reforms to the health and pension systems were introduced, and an unemployment insurance mechanism was created. The emphasis on social rights was to be welcomed over an approach of social benefits as a by-product of aggregate economic growth and social expenditure stuck with the ideal of perfect targeting. Whatever the merits and good intentions of the partial social reforms of the 2000s, these attempts were in the end constrained by the economic power of interest groups that would have been affected by genuinely equitable and democratic social reforms. The profit motive still dominates, without real counterweight, provisions for education, health, and pensions by the private sector in spite of growing social criticism and lack of legitimacy. In fact, an emerging mass of beneficiaries is demanding new social-service delivery systems more oriented toward serving the people than earning profits.

In this line, the high concentration of the market controlled by a reduced number of companies that manage pension funds and the private provision of health services was left virtually unchallenged by the last reform of pensions. Boosting effective competition and starting some social control of the management of the savings of the working poor and the middle class for old age was postponed indefinitely. Unemployment insurance was created but only for workers in the formal private sector. The new system excluded by design employees in the public sector and informal workers. The new system, however, is overburdened by multiple previous problems of access to insurance benefits, badly needed at times of economic and natural hardships.

The labor market remains an area of conflicting views. The neoliberal approach stresses the need for labor flexibility, moderation in wages, and reduced social benefits to boost competitiveness and to keep the profit rate at a high level. Of course, this also enhances the control capital owners have over the labor force and reduces the autonomy of workers. The labor union movement, in contrast, has been demanding further workers' rights, the augmentation of the scope for collective bargaining, and more-balanced capital-labor relations. The Chilean labor market, in spite of the modernization of the productive structure, still exhibits significant degrees of informalization, a lack of labor contracts, considerable differences in pay between men and women, and large differences in pay between large corporations and micro, small, and medium-size firms.

7

Concentration of Economic Power

The New Elites of the Super-Rich, Oligopolistic Markets, and Dual Production Structures

Introduction

As we have shown in previous chapters, the free-market revolution undergone by the Chilean economy in the past three decades changed its social and production structures in various ways, as well as its patterns of wealth distribution. The general trend has been toward concentration in the ownership of production assets and economic polarization in several dimensions: income, wealth, market shares, production structures, and geographic distribution of economic activity along the territory of Chile.[1] This chapter takes a look at three dimensions of economic concentration in Chile: wealth, market shares, and the production structures.

Chile's pattern of economic growth along free-market lines led to the formation of new powerful economic elites associated with finance, retail, manufacturing, services, mining, and other activities. This economic elite can be defined in broad terms as formed by large owners, investors, managers, financiers, and the techno-structure of the private sector. These elites have privileged access to own funds, credit, new technologies, foreign markets, and the ruling political class. The large economic conglomerates of Chile that hold an important part of national productive wealth belong, of course, to the economic elite. The economic elites have assets, purchasing power, and political influence and ownership of the mass media well beyond the average citizen of the country.[2]

---

[1] See Solimano and Torche (2008) and Solimano (2009).
[2] The concept of elites was developed by the "Italian school." Main representatives of this school were Vilfredo Pareto (1848–1923), an economist and sociologist, and the political scientist Gaetano Mosca (1858–1941). On the other side of the Atlantic,

The textbook ideal of a free-market economy of atomistic markets and dispersed economic power that was behind the postulates of Friedman and Hayek and for which Chile was an experimental field of application has been replaced by the reality of a form of capitalism with high degrees of concentrated of economic power in influential and powerful elites. The challenge is how to move to a more equitable distribution of economic assets and power and a more participatory economy in Chile.[3]

In the production sphere, there is a growing differentiation among firms of different size. In fact, it is apparent that the gulf between small and medium-size enterprises, which account for nearly 80 percent of employment creation but a much lower percentage of output generation, and large firms, which are more capital-intensive but generate the bulk of output, exports, and pay higher wages than small and medium size enterprises has not declined and may well have widened. Large firms also are financially and organizationally capable of undertaking large and ambitious investment plans. The bulk of the export base of Chile, its engine of growth, is carried out by large firms, excluding even CODELCO, the state-owned producer and exporter of copper. As discussed in Chapter 3, the economic elites have an important control not only of productive assets but also of the media (TV, newspapers, and radio) and largely own the main private universities. The conservative media and the private

---

the American sociologist C. Wright-Mills, in *The Power Elite* (1956, [2000]), expanded the concept to include the economic, political, and military "power elite" in the United States.

[3] There is a long tradition of promoting less concentrated capitalism and alternative forms of economic organization. This includes various strands. One is associated with the writings of G.K. Chesterton and Hilaire Belloc – distributism – in which assets and property are widely distributed among people rather than within the state (as in bureaucratic socialism) or in a small economic elite (as in highly concentrated capitalism). This doctrine is coincident with the economic views of the Catholic Church as expressed in the encyclical *Rerum Novarum* of Pope Leo XIII. Another brand of social democracy and democratic socialism is the cooperative movement, including the kibbutzim movement in Israel, self-managed enterprises in socialist Yugoslavia, the Mondragon cooperative in Spain, and workers' participation in the boards of companies in Nordic countries and post-apartheid South Africa. A more modern version of the third way was that of Tony Blair, who initially generated hopes for economic and social renewal but who ultimately became discredited when he embraced both former prime minister Margaret Thatcher's economic policies and George W. Bush's foreign adventures in Iraq and other places.

university system help to manufacture a common sense or manufactured consent (in Chomsky's terminology) that steers Chilean society in a direction that preserves the status quo and the influence of the elites and the maintenance of the economic model. As we saw in the previous chapter, at specific junctures, this status quo has also been challenged by the student movement, public opinion, organized labor, and civil society organizations that have asked for democratic reforms in education and are sensitive to big projects with negative environmental impact. The most serious challenge has taken place in 2011.

Wealth Concentration and the Chilean Super-Rich

The process of economic concentration and polarization in Chile has not escaped the pattern observed in many economies in recent decades of a skyrocketing concentration of wealth in the hands of a relatively few individuals and families.

In fact, some twenty-five years ago *Forbes* magazine started to compile a list of the "super-rich," a small elite that owns disproportionate financial and productive wealth in the world economy. *Forbes* first focused on the super-rich in the United States and then expanded its compilation to other countries. According to this publication, there were 1,210 billionaires in the world in 2010, with a combined wealth of US$4.5 trillion. The threshold used by *Forbes* to define billionaires (or super-rich) is a net worth of US$1 billion. In contrast with the gigantic wealth of the 1,210 *Forbes* billionaires, we have more than 2 billion individuals living on less than US$2 a day. This demonstrates the abysmal disparities in the world economy today. The super-rich have accumulated their wealth in sectors such as information technology and communications, oil, banking and finance, real estate, and entertainment. The net worth of the super-rich includes physical and financial assets, real estate, and valuable art objects (human capital is not included as a measure of wealth).

Forbes identifies four Chileans (individuals or families) who belong to the selected group of the world super-rich: Ms. Luksic and family, with a net wealth of US$19.2 billion (with interests in mining, TV, radio and the financial sector); Mr. Horst Paulmann (retail), with

US$10.5 billion; Mr. Eliodoro Matte and family, with US$10.4 billion (forestry and energy); and Mr. Sebastian Piñera (blind fund), with US$2.4 billion. Incidentally, Mr. Piñera is currently the president of Chile for the period 2010–14. The combined wealth of these four individuals and families (in a country with a total population of nearly 17 million) is more than US$42.5 billion (representing approximately 21 percent of GDP in 2010).[4]

It is interesting to note from Table 7.1 that between 2009 (a recession year) and 2010, the net wealth of the two wealthiest families in Chile – the Luksic family and Horst Paulmann and family – almost *doubled*. In fact, the Luksic family saw its wealth jump from US$11 billion to nearly US$20 billion, and the Paulmann family increased its wealth from US$5 billion to US$10.5 billion over the same period. In turn, the four families increased their wealth by 62 percent between 2009 and 2010 according to *Forbes*. This high polarization and concentration in wealth levels in Chile is unprecedented in recent decades.[5] [6]

The rise of the elite super-rich in Chile and throughout the world points to the basic question of whether these huge fortunes are due solely to ingenuity, hard work, bright ideas, superb education, and good luck in competitive markets (that is, what could be considered rewards for talent and merit). Reality seems more complex than that, however. In several cases around the world, prominent individuals on the *Forbes* list were granted special licenses to run business monopolies and had access to special subsidies, tariff protections, and subsidized credits. In other cases, the lucky individuals were allowed to privatize, at a cheap price or no price at all, formerly state-owned enterprises in noncompetitive and nontransparent ways. The economic rewards of having the right political and social connections can be huge in some cases.

---

[4] As a reference point, in 2007 the United States had 406 billionaires in a population of 300 million, whose combined wealth amounted to approximately 10 percent of U.S. GDP. Wealth is much more concentrated in Chile than in the United States.

[5] Just as a comparison, the average wage in Chile increased by 1.7 percent in real terms in 2010 (December to December).

[6] On a global scale, in 2010 the selected group of super-rich was headed by Carlos Slim from Mexico, with US$74 billion, followed by Bill Gates (US$56 billion), Warren Buffet (US$50 billion), and others from the former Soviet Union (101 billionaires), "communist" China (115 billionaires), India (55 billionaires), and other nations.

Chile and the Neoliberal Trap

Table 7.1. *Just Four Individuals (Families) Have an*
Overwhelming Share of Chilean Wealth (in Millions US$)

Individuals	Year					Forbes Ranking
	2006	2007	2008	2009	2010	
Andrónico Luksic[1]	-	10,000	6,000	11,000	19,200	27
Anacleto Angelini[2]	6,000	1,000	-	-	-	-
Horst Paulmann and Family	-	-	-	5,000	10,500	75
Eliodoro Matte and Family	5,600	7,900	5,900	8,100	10,400	77
Sebastián Piñera	1,200	1,300	1,000	2,200	2,400	488
Total of the Four Major Fortunes	12,800	20,200	12,900	26,300	42,500	
Chile's GDP (in Current Billions, USD)	147	164	174	162	204	
Four Major Fortunes as % of GDP	8.7	12.3	7.4	16.2	20.8	

[1] Mr. Luksic died in August 2005; fortune inherited by his widow, Ms. Iris Fontbona, and family.
[2] Mr. Angelini died in August 2007; fortune inherited by his widow, Ms. Maria Noseda Zambra.
Source: Author's own elaboration on the basis of data from *Forbes* magazine and the Central Bank of Chile.

Market Concentration

Another form of economic concentration is increasing market shares in key activities. This refers to the high participation of a few companies in the total sales or production of a certain market. A high degree of market concentration by a few firms has the potential capacity to generate big profits and to accumulate wealth, enabling capital to be reproduced and expanded. In addition, markets dominated by a few firms often leads to a higher price than competitive equilibrium, generating a loss of consumer surplus and a level of production that is inferior to that of the competitive equilibrium, generating a corresponding loss of productive efficiency.[7] In order to have some empirical assessment of the degree of market concentration in key industries in Chile, a country considered to entertain relatively small markets that can lead to this concentration, we shall use the Herfindahl-Hirschman Index (HHI), which is calculated by adding each company's squared market participation. The HHI can take values between zero and one. If the HHI value is closer to one, the degree of market concentration is high; in contrast, if it is closer to zero, the market is very competitive. This index is based on theoretical models of oligopoly, using information from companies that participate in the market. The index gives greater weight to larger companies.

The HHI is calculated for six sectors: forestry, pharmacies, banking, pension fund administration, mining, and health insurance. The definition of market concentration used in the United States to evaluate if the merging of companies can lead to increased degrees of market concentration is the following: a sector is qualified as nonconcentrated if the HHI is less than 0.1, it is moderately concentrated if the HHI is between 0.1 and 0.18, it is highly concentrated if the HHI index is higher than 0.18. Calculating the HHI with 2008 data for Chile, we find that the six analyzed sectors are located between moderately concentrated and highly concentrated: *no* sector of the six chosen can be classified as nonconcentrated according to the definition adopted in

---

[7] According to the theory of contestable markets, a market's level of concentration is not always an indicator of noncompetitive market structures. In fact, Baumol, Panzar, and Willig (1988) have shown, in a theoretical model, that in the absence of entrance or exit costs, the market is "contestable" and works in a competitive way, regardless of the degree of concentration. The intuition is that if the existing company (incumbent) raises its price over the marginal costs and gains supranormal profits in a market with no entry or exit costs, the new entries will try to own these profits, to which the company's response will be to lower its prices to competitive levels in order to prevent the entrance of these new competitors. Therefore, a very concentrated market could theoretically operate as a competitive market. In reality, however, the conditions for a market to be "contestable" are very strict, and the level of market concentration is still an important consideration in competitive policies. In fact, increasingly, mergers of companies are considered to be potential reducers of competition in already concentrated markets (see Agostini, 2008).

the United States. The specific results are as follows (the value of the HHI is in parenthesis):

1. Highly concentrated sectors: pharmacies (0.30) and pension fund administration companies (0.22)
2. Moderately concentrated sectors (HHI): health insurance institutions (0.18), mining (0.15), banking (0.13), and forestry (0.13)

The most concentrated sectors are pharmacies, with three main chains dominating the market,[8] and pension fund administration companies (AFPs), with six companies in the market. It should not escape attention that these two highly concentrated sectors operate in critical activities from the viewpoint of human welfare and economic security: the first provide drugs and medicines important for the health of the population, and the second are privately manage pension funds for the retirement of millions of Chileans.[9] In turn, health insurance institutions (ISAPRES) have a degree of concentration close to the level that is considered highly concentrated (0.177). The evolution over time of the level of concentration is displayed in Figure 7.1, panels A to F.

It is worth noting that pharmacies, forestry, pension fund administration companies, and health insurance institutions have all *increased* their level of market concentration during the first decade of the twenty-first century according to the HHI. In turn, during this period, the degree of concentration has remained more or less constant in mining and banking. It is interesting to note the significant degree of market concentration in sectors that are regulated by the state through the respective superintending organizations, which speaks of the difficulties in effectively regulating sectors wielding high economic power and political clout. In this connection, it is worth noting that the growing consolidation of the private pension system occurred in the past two decades or so, as already mentioned in Chapter 6: whereas there were twenty-two AFPs in 1994, the number fell to five in 2008, then grew to six in 2009 after the reform of the pension system. This pale increase of just one (small) AFP was claimed to be evidence that the reform "boosted competitiveness" in the AFP market.

[8] A proven case of price collusion between the pharmaceutical chains and providers was sanctioned by the judiciary in Chile in 2010.
[9] More than 4 million Chileans make active contributions to the AFP system (more than 8 million belong to the system), and approximately 800,000 receive pensions.

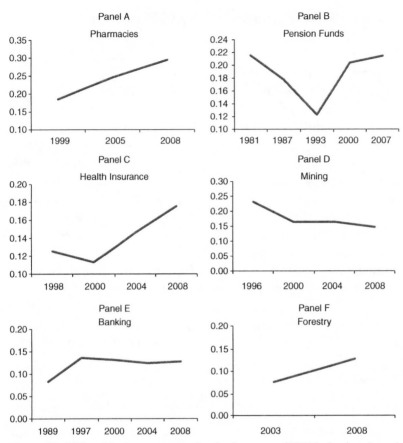

Figure 7.1 Chile – Market concentration in six sectors (HHI index in selected years).
Source: The author's own elaboration based on information from private industry associations and superintendencies, via websites.

Concentration and Heterogeneity of the Production Structure

Another indicator of the highly differentiated economic structure of Chile is the heterogeneity of its production structure. This heterogeneity is reflected in significant differences in capital intensity, employment generation, technology development, export capacity, and innovation between large companies and small and medium-size companies (SME) and micro enterprises. As indicated before, larger companies have much larger market shares in production, sales, exports, and expenditures in innovation (when relevant).[10] A structural feature of the SME is that it is a labor-intensive sector and therefore can be an important source of income and jobs generation for many people in society. In fact, the micro, small, and medium-size companies are important sources of employment and income generators for the middle and working classes, which can help improve income distribution and reduce wealth concentration and market shares of large firms.[11]

The SME sector is often squeezed by the paying practices of buyers (public and private) and the types of contracts established with them by big corporations to which small-business supply inputs and services. Payment delays by contractors and other disadvantageous conditions for SME sector are routine in Chile. The SMEs face various handicaps when trying to grow: limited access to credit and expensive working capital, disadvantages in market access, backward technological platforms, and excessive time spent dealing with the bureaucracies that grant permits and licenses.[12] In many countries,

---

[10] An important difference between large and small companies is their access to credit and other sources of financing. The financial markets generally operate with asymmetric information between credit suppliers and applicants. Credit suppliers generally have less information on the loan-repayment capacity and real economic viability of companies than those who apply for credit. This point was raised by Stiglitz and Weiss (1981), who proved that increasing credit costs (higher interest rates) could be an inefficient mechanism to distinguish between good and bad debtors. It is important to highlight that information asymmetries have a larger effect on smaller companies, where their balances and information in general are less developed and systematized than in larger companies. Another factor that inhibits making loans to smaller companies, encouraging banks to concentrate on a portfolio of larger companies, is the size of the credit operations. If banks want to serve small and medium-size companies, they must reduce the size of their credits, which leads to dividing the fixed costs of collecting information and client analysis amongst smaller operations. This makes it less profitable for the bank from a private point of view – to give credit to smaller companies.

[11] The increase in the relative participation of small and medium-size companies seems to be an empirical regularity as the level of development in different countries increases. The Ayyagari et al. (2005) study, which used a sample of seventy-six economies of different income levels, discovered that the participation of small and medium-size companies in the product and employment areas of the manufacturing sector increases as the income level per capita increases in that country. Also, the informal sector's participation in the employment and product areas decreases as the income level per capita increases.

[12] International and historic evidence demonstrates that there are important differences in the access to bank financing between small and medium-size companies and large companies. In general, firms' internal financing (retained profits) and informal sources of credit are more important financial mechanisms in small and

including the United States, the state is an important buyer of products of the SME sector, and industrial promotion of this sector is carried out through the small business administrations.[13] In contrast, in Chile it is not a priority for the state to make purchases in the SME sector.

Empirical Evidence of the Heterogeneity of the Chilean Production Structure: Micro, Small, Medium-Size, and Large Companies

The empirical evidence provided below confirms the presumption that Chile has a very heterogeneous production structure as far as company size, access to credit, participation in international markets, and capital intensity goes.[14] This heterogeneity and production concentration mimics the highly unequal income distribution documented in this book. There are two main sources of data regarding firm size. One is a survey of socioeconomic characteristics of households, CASEN, which classifies firm size according to employment level; a second source is the Chilean Internal Revenue Service (SII), which classifies firm size by level of sales.

medium-size companies than in large companies. The World Bank did a study on sources of company financing for thirty-eight countries in Latin America, Africa, Asia, and Europe (carried out with data from the biennium 2002–3). The study found that smaller companies base their financing on two sources: (1) internal resources such as retained profits and (2) sources from families, friends, and informal loaners. The importance of banking credit (external financing) as a financing source for medium-size and small companies is significantly less than internal sources, although there have been some significant differences detected among the companies that have been studied. The use of commercial credit of supplies, credit cards, and leasing is relatively low but of certain importance in some countries. Finally, this study has discovered that access to external sources of financing is related to the level of development of the financial markets and the level of economic development of those countries. Therefore, it is more likely that small and medium-size companies in developed countries and countries with medium to high incomes have more access to banking credit than companies in countries with small and medium incomes. The territorial dimension of the financing sources was (and still is) important in these countries.

[13] See Solimano, Pollack, Weiner, and Wurgaft (2007) for a discussion of policies to promote SMEs in the United States and other countries and their relevance for Chile.

[14] See Infante and Sunkel (2009) for a heterogeneity analysis using the input-output matrix for Chile.

The CASEN survey's size classification of firms is as follows:

- Micro firms: between 1 and 9 employees
- Small firms: between 10 and 49 employees
- Medium-size firms: between 50 and 199 employees
- Large firms: more than 200 employees

The SII uses the level of "annual sales net of value-added tax, VAT, defined in a monetary unit of constant value (UF)."[15]

- Micro firms: productive units with sales up to 2.400 UF
- Small firms: productive units with sales between 2.401 UF and 25.000 UF
- Medium-size firms: productive units with sales between 25.001 and 100.000 UF
- Large firms: productive units with sales of more than 100.000 UF

It is worth noting that the CASEN survey lists more companies than those included in the SII register in the category of micro enterprises, because the CASEN survey includes informal micro production units, which may not be legally registered and do not pay first-category taxes (and thus are excluded from the SII register).[16]

Table 7.2 shows that micro and small firms are very labor intensive (CASEN survey), representing almost 64 percent of total employment. The contribution of the segment of micro and small firms to total sales is much lower, however, reaching only 10.5 percent (SII's definition).

Medium-size and large firms generate 36 percent of total employment and 89.5 percent of sales. Using the sales criteria (SII), although medium-size and large firms represent only 4 percent of the total number of firms, they generate 89.5 percent of sales. These numbers provide evidence that despite being less numerous, medium-size and large companies make a large contribution to sales but a relatively modest contribution to total employment. This generates a sort of dual production structure with important differences in labor productivity and wage rates among firms of different sizes. In turn, micro and small firms

---

[15] UF stands for Unidad de Fomento, a currency denomination unit that adjusts daily by the rate of change of the Consumer Price Index. In January 2011, one UF was equivalent to US$40.

[16] It may be possible that the number of "micro firms" according to the CASEN survey may be classified as "small companies" using the SII's sales-level criteria.

Table 7.2. *Chile: Employment, Number of Firms, and Sales by Company Size, 2006–2007*

Company Size	Companies and Employment, CASEN 2006		Companies and Sales, SII Criterion (2007)		
	Employment	% of Total	No. of Companies	% of Total	% of Total Sales [a]
Microenterprise	2,300,697	45.7	585,225	78.8	2.6
Small Firms	920,840	18.3	128,043	17.2	7.9
Micro and Small Firms	3,221,537	63.9	713,268	96.0	10.5
Medium-size Firms	699,078	13.9	19,469	2.6	7.9
Large Firms	1,118,896	22.2	10,171	1.4	81.6
Medium-size and Large Firms	1,817,974	36.1	29,640	4.0	89.5
TOTAL	5,039,511	100	742,908	100	100

Note: (a): Values from 2005.
Source: CASEN Surveys 2006 and SII (Chilean Customs Office and SII).

are mainly concentrated in the business sector (retail and wholesale), services, agriculture, and transportation. In contrast, medium-size and large firms are relatively important in construction, mining, and the financial sector (see Table 7.3).

As mentioned before, an important source of economic growth in Chile is generated by the export sector, which is part of the country's outward-oriented development strategy. What types of companies dominate the export business? According to the information provided in Table 7.4, the share of micro, small, and medium-size firms that make sales in the export markets is small, between 4 and 5 percent. In contrast, large firms make up the bulk of exports (between 95 percent and 96 percent of total exports between the years 1999 and 2003). These numbers, however, may somewhat underrepresent the indirect importance of small and medium-size firms in the export sector to the extent that the SMEs are also providers of goods, services, and intermediate parts and inputs to large firms that have the capacity to serve international markets through exports.

Table 7.3. *Sector and Size Distribution of the Number of Formal
Companies, in Percentages, 2003 (SII Criterion)*

Sector	Micro	Small	Micro and Small	Medium	Large	Medium and Large	Total
Trade	43,6	32,4	41,9	34,9	32,4	34,1	41,6
Service	12,9	16,0	13,4	14,8	10,3	13,3	13,4
Transport	11,1	13,3	11,5	8,7	6,6	8,0	11,4
Agricultural	11,5	10,2	11,3	7,1	4,7	6,4	11,1
Industry	6,7	10,3	7,2	12,9	17,8	14,5	7,5
Financial	5,3	7,6	5,7	9,9	14,2	11,3	5,9
Construction	5,0	7,9	5,4	9,0	8,8	8,9	5,5
Mining	0,2	0,5	0,3	0,8	1,6	1,0	0,3
Other	3,7	1,9	3,4	2,0	3,7	2,5	3,4
TOTAL	100	100	100	100	100	100	100

Source: Author's own elaboration based on data from "La Situación de la Micro y Pequeña Empresa en Chile," Chile Emprende, Government of Chile, 2005.

Table 7.4. *Percentage Share of Exports by Company Size,
1999–2003*

Year	Micro and Small	Medium	Large	Total
1999	1.8	3.5	94.7	100
2000	1.7	3.1	95.2	100
2001	1.5	3.4	95.1	100
2002	1.4	3.2	95.4	100
2003	1.3	2.6	96.1	100

Source: Author's own elaboration based on data from Chilean Customs Office and SII, 2003.

Finally, evidence shows that there is a territorial concentration in medium-size and large companies in the Metropolitan Region, in comparison with micro and small companies that have a relatively even distribution – slightly lower in the Metropolitan Region and higher in the Maule Region (VII Region), as shown in Figure 7.2, panels A and B.

In summary, the information reviewed highlights the fact that micro and small companies are important sources of employment generation but that their contribution to total value added and exports is rather small. In contrast, medium-size and large companies have a

Panel A

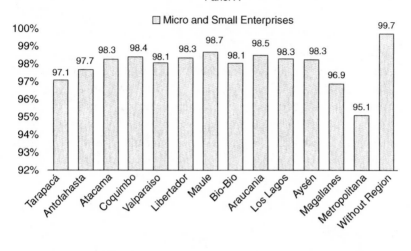

Panel B

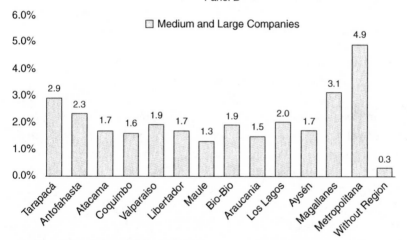

Figure 7.2 Chile – Regional distribution of firms by size (2003, SII criterion).
Source: The author's own elaboration based on data from "La Situación de la
Micro y Pequeña Empresa en Chile," Chile Emprende, Government of Chile,
2005.

low relative contribution to total employment, but their contribution to exports and total value added is high. Small and medium-size organizations are much more oriented toward the internal market than are large companies and are more evenly distributed across the national territory than are large companies, which are concentrated in the Metropolitan Region. Therefore, a development strategy that promotes a less geographically concentrated income distribution would expand the internal market and elicit a supply response from small and medium-size enterprises, which are the main generators of employment and income for the poor and middle class.

Concluding Remarks

This chapter has taken a look at the patterns of economic concentration and uneven development in the Chilean economy as demonstrated in three dimensions: high concentration of wealth and the emergence of a small minority of super-rich that controls a disproportionately high share of national wealth; a significant concentration of market participation in banking, pharmaceuticals, health insurance, pension fund management, and others by relatively few firms and conglomerates that enjoy high market shares; and the existence of a production structure in which the segment of micro, small, and medium-size enterprises generates the bulk of employment, but their contribution to total value added is low because of relatively low productivity compared with large firms. In addition, the export market is dominated by large firms. A new, socially inclusive development strategy must stimulate the sector of small and medium-size enterprises that are employment intensive and provide the main source of income for the middle and working classes. This new development strategy should strengthen the capacity of the Chilean state to regulate and reduce the enormous degree of concentration of big corporations and also incorporate the largely forgotten dimension of achieving a more even geographic distribution of economic activity and wealth generation. Chile is a very centralistic country in which most of the economic activity is generated in the capital city of Santiago and the Metropolitan Region, to the detriment of the county's other regions, which have a reduced voice in decisions at the national level that affect both their own populations and the country as a whole.

8

Limits to Chilean Democracy and Governance for Capital

Introduction

The current post-authoritarian Chilean democracy is to a large extent the result of the country's turbulent history during the past four decades. It is also influenced, however, by the evolution of the political system of the past two centuries as an independent nation. Compared with other Latin American nations, Chile is often considered a case of democratic continuity, if we measure that as a low frequency of presidential crises during most of the twentieth century. In the past fifty years, the "only" extra-constitutional interruption was the military coup of September 1973, led by General Augusto Pinochet against President Salvador Allende, democratically elected in 1970. Furthermore, contrary to the myth of an always exemplary democracy are the main landmarks that have shaped the Chilean political system in the nineteenth and twentieth centuries, such as the constitutions of 1833, 1925, and 1980, which did not emerge from fully democratic conditions. These constitutions – as representative of social contracts – were not deliberated by democratically elected constitutional assemblies. Instead they were drafted by special commissions appointed by the executive power of the time, often supported by the military, to get constitutional texts aligned with their political interests. Moreover, the approval procedures in plebiscites of limited validity were not exactly a standard of high democracy.[1]

The restoration of democracy after the end of the Pinochet regime in the early 1990s gave rise to a democracy quite different from the

---

[1] See Salazar (2009) and Gomez-Leyton (2010).

pre-1973 political regime. Its basic contours were conditioned by the compromises made by the opposition to the Pinochet regime in its later phase. That opposition shifted from a position of seeking the replacement of the Pinochet constitution of 1980 to reforming some provisos of the prevailing constitution, which would bring an end to the authoritarian period and permit democratic elections. As part of that negotiation, the military requested that General Pinochet become permanent commander in chief of the army after stepping down as president and that no formal legal investigations be conducted of the massive violations of human rights that occurred in the authoritarian period (except in some cases of special notoriety).[2]

It is apparent that the consolidation of the economic model during the past thirty years became an absolute priority for both the military regime and the democratic administrations (albeit with a greater somewhat social focus for the latter) and that this was another condition in the negotiation for the end of the military regime. The free-market economic model required a society with a low level of political participation and weak labor unions and civil society organizations. It also had to be one in which the ordinary citizens have a very limited capacity to question and challenge the process of capital accumulation and expansion of the influence of capital not only in its traditional economic spheres (production, trade, finance) but also in the provision of education and health services, the administration of pension funds, the ownership of the media by single families, the creation of private universities, and so on. It is fair to say that the most influential interest groups in the definition of public policies have been banking and business associations helped by a technocracy of economists enthralled with neoliberal economics.

As discussed in Chapter 3, the plan to build a market economy eventually turned into a plan for a market society, using the apt description of Karl Polanyi (1944). As also discussed in Chapter 3, the cementing of a market society required a cultural revolution that would create a new "common sense" that would give legitimacy to the new economic order (besides the demobilization of civil society and social movements). The main focus of the authorities of the post-Pinochet

---

[2] As noted in Chapter 2, however, a nontrial truth commission was established by President Aylwin to clarify the extent and conditions of such violations.

transition was not in the deepening of democracy but in the assurance of good governance for private investment to support economic growth and prosperity (and ensure handsome profits for capital). In this chapter, we shall present data on governance.

Features of Chilean Democracy after the Pinochet Regime

The Chilean democracy of the 1990s and 2000s has been of "low intensity" in terms of participation of civil society in decision making. The youth, in contrast with previous decades, have been reluctant to participate in party politics, and their turnout in national elections has been low. Also, Chileans living outside the country – the diaspora largely associated with the Chilean exile during Pinochet's regime, besides those living abroad for economic and professional reasons – are still, twenty years after the restoration of democracy, not allowed to vote in Chilean elections. Thus, the post-authoritarian democracy has maintained certain important anomalies.

The Partially Reformed Constitution of 1980 Is Still Ruling
The 1980 constitution approved by a plebiscite and held without electoral register, under a controlled press and curtailed civil liberties, provided a legal framework for the military regime of General Pinochet and guided the transition to a restricted democracy in Chile. The 1980 constitution replaced the constitution of 1925, which was in effect until 1973. The 1980 constitution protected the primacy of private property over state ownership and later through the binomial system ensured the exclusion of non-*Concertacion* left-wing political parties and other independent political movements. The new constitution legally asserted the role of the armed forces in the Chilean political system and restricted the role of the popular vote in some key political decisions. The constitution made it very difficult for the state to create enterprises and left virtually no room for calling a plebiscite on matters of first importance for the country. In view of the evidently undemocratic nature of these provisos, a constitutional reform was undertaken in 2005 during the Lagos administration. As discussed in Chapter 2, these reforms were never put forward for ratification by a national plebiscite and were not preceded by a wide process of discussion by the citizenship. The 2005 reforms eliminated the appointed

senators and reduced the national security council's powers, but they fell short of replacing the authoritarian constitution of 1980 by a new constitutional charter.

An Army-"Protected" Democracy (1990–2005)

This constitution of 1980 promoted the notion of a "protected democracy" by making the armed forces the "guarantors of the institutional order" and granting them a constitutional role in Chilean politics through the national security council; in addition, it placed various restrictions on civilian governance of the army. In fact, civilian presidents could not remove the commander in chief of the army without the consent of the national security council, a proviso eliminated in 2005, enabling the removal of the commanders only after reporting to the upper chamber of parliament. As a witness to the influence and power of the military over Chilean society, several years after leaving the presidency of the country, General Pinochet continued as commander in chief of the Chilean army, part of the senate was not chosen by popular vote (the *senadores designados*, or appointed-senators system), and the national security council retained important powers. Another indication of the influence and privileges of the armed forces in the new democracy is the fact that, at the time of the writing of this book, the Chilean armed forces still receive 10 percent of the gross revenues of the state-owned copper company, CODELCO. As indicated before, this allocation is not subject to oversight from congress and is not subject to the transparency laws that apply to the civilian public sector.[3] Besides, the personnel of the armed forces maintained their own pension system, CAPREDENA (Caja de Previsión de la Defensa Nacional). Army officers and their families do not have to enroll in the AFP, the private social security system, as do the rest of the civilian population. Before the pension reforms of 1981, several employees of the public sector, the central bank, and other entities had their own *cajas de prevision*, a feature that was eliminated with the reform of the social security system that year.

---

[3] As mentioned in Chapter 1, the level of defense spending in Chile, 3.5 percent of GDP, is among the highest in Latin America. An initiative of the Piñera government is attempting to abolish this reserved law. As of the writing of this book, this initiative has not yet gone to congress.

The Binominal Electoral System

The binominal electoral system in Chile was introduced after Pinochet's defeat in the October 1988 plebiscite, when the military junta approved Law 18,799 (the Constitutional Organic Law on Popular Elections and Vote Counting). The title of the law is both accurate and disingenuous – it is meant to ensure a speedy, fecund process for policymaking and legislation, but it is not a fertile ground for broad-based popular participation in the process.

The procedure for allocating seats in the congress after a vote is the following. In order for a party or coalition to win both seats in a district, it must double the vote of its nearest competitor. A party need garner only 33.4 percent of the vote to obtain one seat and must win 66.7 percent of the vote to win two. Hence, if the highest-polling coalition or party wins 66.6 percent of the vote and its nearest competitor receives 33.4 percent, each wins one seat, or 50 percent of the total seats in the district. The electoral system just described was intended to make it very difficult for parties and political movements that do not belong to the two main political coalitions (the Concertación de Partidos por la Democracia and the Coalición por el Cambio, formerly Alianza for Chile) to achieve representation in parliament. Under the binomial system, between 1990 and 2010 the following parties outside the two coalitions did not have representation in congress and the chamber of deputies: the Chilean Communist Party (in early 1973, this party had a peak vote of almost 15 percent of the electorate), the Humanist Party, the Christian-Left Party, and the Green Party. In 2010, the Communist Party returned to parliament's lower house, electing three representatives to the chamber of deputies after entering into an electoral pact with the Concertación. A consequence of the binominal system is that legislation proposed by the center-left governments in the 1990s and 2000s was negotiated in parliament only with the center-right political parties, as no representatives of the (non-Concertación) political left and ecological and regionalist movements had representatives in parliament, a feature that has tilted legislation toward more conservative postures.

Nonelected Senators (1990–2005)

Another very peculiar feature of the post-Pinochet transition in Chile, embedded in the constitution of 1980, was the presence of a group of appointed (nonelected) senators in congress. This practice was in place from 1990 (when the National Congress was reopened) until 2006, a year after the approval of the constitutional reforms of 2005. Between 1990 and 2006, the senate was composed by thirty-eight elected senators, nine designated senators, and two "senators for life" (one of them being General Pinochet), totaling forty-nine senators.

The president appointed two nonelected senators, one required to be a former university rector and one a former minister of state. The supreme court appointed three nonelected senators. The national security council designated four senators, each of whom had to be a former commander of the army, national police (Carabineros), navy, or air force, and have held that post for at least two years. One senator must be chosen from each of the four services.

The rationale for designating these nonelected senators was that they would not be tied to any particular constituency nor would face reelection, and so they would be able to put "the interests of the nation as a whole ahead of the interests of a particular political sector." Needless to say, the justification was a veil for an undemocratic process that ensured a stacked senate vote on any piece of legislation. The system was finally eliminated in the constitutional reform of 2005 and approved by parliament, along with the restrictions on the civilian presidents in appointing and removing the commander in chief of the army. Nevertheless, as explained in Chapter 2, nonelected senators did *not* really disappear. After 2006, political parties could appoint, without having to resort to popular vote, senators or lower-chamber representatives in case they resigned to take up a ministerial or other high-level position in the executive branch of government.

Democracy, Authoritarian Cycles, and Presidential Crises in Chile and Other Latin American Countries

Let us review some comparative empirical evidence to verify the hypothesis of the assumed stability of Chilean democracy compared with other Latin American countries. As shown in Chapter 2, violence and authoritarianism are features that have not been absent in the past 200 hundred years of Chilean history.

The past forty to fifty years in Latin America have been characterized by cycles of authoritarianism and democracy. The last wave of authoritarian regimes affected several Latin American Southern Cone countries in the 1960s, 1970s, and 1980s. During those years, military regimes in Brazil, Argentina, Uruguay, and Chile sought to shrink and control the opposition in universities, labor unions, political parties, and suppressing civil liberties. In various cases, these regimes set those countries back economically. An attempt to measure the incidence of military and semi-democratic regimes in Latin America is shown in Table 8.1, drawn from Solimano (2010b). The greatest number of semi-democratic and nondemocratic regimes between the 1960s and the 1990s were concentrated in Argentina, Chile, and Ecuador in the period 1960–2006. Moreover, it is estimated that the breakdown in constitutional government was most severe in Argentina and Chile, when civil rights and constitutional safeguards for the population were suspended, increasing the vulnerability of individuals to abuses of power by the state, thus prompting, among other things, greater emigration to other countries.[4] Argentina had frequent cycles of democratic, semi-democratic, and authoritarian regimes since the 1930s, and the last military regime, of 1976 to 1983 (one of the most repressive in recent history), followed an increasingly unstable and socially conflictive situation associated with the last government of General Juan Perón and then his widow, Estela Martínez. Both the Argentine and Chilean military juntas were highly repressive anticommunist regimes. In contrast, the national popular military regimes of Ecuador and Peru of the late 1960s and 1970s were far less repressive than the Argentine and Chilean right-wing regimes and much less anticommunist in their rhetoric.

A measure of the frequency of political and presidential crises is presented in Table 8.2. (By presidential crisis, we mean a president who does not finish his or her constitutional term owing to a military coup, a civil uprising, or other political cause.) This table shows a high frequency of presidential crises – an indicator of fragility of the political system – in the period 1950–2008 in Argentina and Bolivia but not in Chile. That table shows that while Argentina had seven presidential crises and Bolivia nineteen, Chile had only one, albeit very severe (the presidential crisis of 1973).[5]

---

[4] See Solimano (2010b) for an analysis of how authoritarian regimes and internal and external conflicts spur emigration, consisting mainly of high human-capital individuals.

[5] Besides showing a high degree of political instability, Bolivia also has high levels of income and wealth inequality. High inequality is also observed in Chile but with more stable political systems. Argentina has lower levels of inequality than Bolivia and lower political stability (judged by the frequency of presidential crises) than Chile.

Table 8.1. *Evolution of Political Regimes in Selected Latin American Countries,* 1960–2006*

Country	Decade	Constitutional Presidents in the Decade	De Facto Presidents in the Decade	Percent of Semi- & Non-Democratic Regimes in the Decade**
Argentina	1960–1969	3	1	35.0
	1970–1979	4	4	32.5
	1980–1989	2	4	34.9
	1990–1999	3	0	0.0
	2000–2006	4	0	0.0
Chile	1960–1969	2	0	0.0
	1970–1979	1	1	65.0
	1980–1989	0	1	100.0
	1990–1999	2	0	0.0
	2000–2006	2	0	0.0
Colombia	1960–1969	3	0	0.0
	1970–1979	4	0	0.0
	1980–1989	3	0	0.0
	1990–1999	4	0	0.0
	2000–2006	2	0	0.0
Ecuador	1960–1969	5	2	42.5
	1970–1979	2	2	65.0
	1980–1989	4	0	0.0
	1990–1999	5	0	0.0
	2000–2006	4	0	0.0
Dominican Republic	1960–1969	9	5	21.8
	1970–1979	2	0	0.0
	1980–1989	4	0	0.0
	1990–1999	2	0	0.0
	2000–2006	3	0	0.0

Notes:
* Counts the number of presidents holding office in each decade.
** In a "democracy," authorities are elected by universal vote, and civil liberties and political rights are respected. In a "nondemocratic" regime, political authorities take power by extra-constitutional means. In "semi-democratic" regimes, the normal functioning of democracy is interrupted; these can be "self-coups" and entail, for example, the dissolution of parliament and restrictions on the freedom of the press and civil liberties, but other civil liberties may remain and some independent political powers may still operate.
Source: Solimano (2010b).

Table 8.2. *Presidential Crises in Argentina, Bolivia, and Chile*

Indicators		Argentina	Bolivia	Chile
Government Type		Presidential System	Presidential System	Presidential System
Regional Political Division		Federal	Unitary	Unitary
Number of Political Parties in 2009	National	37	17[a]	13
	Regional	30		
Number of Presidents or Heads of State (1950–2008)		25	28	10
Number of Presidential Crises (1950–2008)[b]		9	17	1
Ascension to Power (1950–2008)	Democratic Election[c]	15	12	8
	Nondemocratic Ascension	12	21	1

Notes:

[a] Refers to fourteen current political parties, one political alliance, and two citizen associations, all of which are allowed to have candidates.

[b] "Presidential crisis" refers to when a president does not finish his or her constitutional term owing to a coup d'etat, a civil uprising, or other political cause.

[c] The sum of democratic and nondemocratic elections is not necessarily the same as the number of presidents, because there are some presidents who keep themselves in power for more than one term.

Sources: Solimano (2005); *Nueva Historia de la Nación Argentina* (7 La Argentina del Siglo XX by La Academia Nacional de la Historia); *Editorial Planeta Argentina S.A.I.C* (Buenos Aires, 2000); http://www.todo-argentina.net/historia/index.htm; http://www.ilustrados.com/publicaciones/EpZplVlkFydSmoFfya.php; http://www.cidob.org/bios/castellano/indices/indices.htm (Argentina); http://www.historiadelpais.com.ar/presidentes.php; http://www.historiadelpais.com.ar/menubio/camden.html; http://www.historicaltextarchive.com/sections.php?op=listarticles&secid=41.

What these results seem to show is that Chile has a tendency for stability in its political regimes. Its democracy, albeit with limitations and peculiarities, tends to be stable. In turn, when the country turned to authoritarian rule, that regime was also quite stable, unless compared with other military regimes in Latin America.

Governance for Capital: Perceptions Indexes

In the previous sections, we have followed a political economy approach to briefly assess the democratic (and undemocratic) nature of the Chilean political system, including its degree of stability and also the frequency of political and democratic crises. A different approach, fashionable in recent years in economics and business literature, has focused on the ability of public institutions and legal systems to foster (or hamper) the development of the private sector (business development, private investment), considered the engine of economic growth.[6] In a way, this new approach, rather than focusing primarily on issues of citizenship, respect for human and workers' rights, and the degree of social participation in democracy, is concerned that the conditions for capital investment be made safe and predictable. This approach has been promoted by international financial institutions such as the World Bank. The World Bank for several years has been publishing an index on the governance conditions of countries based on the opinions of company executives, entrepreneurs, foreign investors, and the general public (see Table 8.4). This qualitative (subjective) index measures six dimensions of the "the quality of institutions and the governance conditions" of a country. These six dimensions are voice and accountability, political stability and absence of violence, government effectiveness, regulatory quality, rule of law, and control of corruption.[7]

The results of Table 8.3 show that Chile tends to be above (scores better than) Argentina, Bolivia, Brazil, and the average of Latin America on the six variables that compose the World Bank's governance index. In dimensions such as voice and accountability and political stability and absence of violence, however, Chile is similar to Costa Rica but

---

[6] The political theory of the costs of transaction (North [1991], Dixit [1996]) provides the analytical framework of this approach combined with a focus on private sector development. An alternative approach to institutions is found in Acemoglu and Robinson (2006), who stress that institutions are also useful in maintaining the power of influential and powerful elite positions as well as the political and economic status quo. This latter idea borrows, not always acknowledged, Marx's notion that institutions are instrumental to the maintenance and consolidation of power of dominant economic classes that own capital.

[7] The six governance indicators are measured in units ranging from -2.5 to 2.5. Higher values (closer to 2.5) correspond to better governance outcomes, and lower values (closer to -2.5) amount to poor governance as measured by the six subjective indicators.

Table 8.3. *Governance Indicators for Chile, Latin American Countries, and OECD, 2009*

	Voice and Account-ability	Political Stability and Absence of Violence	Govern-ment Effective-ness	Regula-tory Quality	Rule of Law	Control of Corrup-tion
Chile	0.96	0.63	1.21	1.50	1.25	1.37
Argentina	0.25	−0.02	−0.42	−0.90	−0.66	−0.49
Bolivia	−0.08	−0.82	−0.72	−0.98	−1.22	−0.71
Brazil	0.51	0.29	0.08	0.18	−0.18	−0.07
Costa Rica	0.97	0.65	0.43	0.53	0.56	0.70
Uruguay	1.10	0.88	0.69	0.37	0.72	1.22
Latin America	0.10	−0.36	−0.23	−0.10	−0.51	−0.27
OECD	1.33	0.90	1.53	1.41	1.48	1.61

Note: The governance indicators presented here reflect the statistical compilation of responses on the quality of governance given by a large number of enterprise, citizen, and expert survey respondents in industrial and developing countries, as reported by a number of survey institutes, think tanks, and nongovernmental and international organizations.

[1] Voice and Accountability (VA) – measures perceptions of the extent to which a country's citizens are able to participate in selecting their government, as well as freedom of expression, freedom of association, and a free media.

[2] Political Stability and Absence of Violence (PV) – measures perceptions of the likelihood that the government will be destabilized or overthrown by unconstitutional or violent means, including politically motivated violence and terrorism.

[3] Government Effectiveness (GE) – measures perceptions of the quality of public services and civil service and the degree of independence from political pressures, the quality of policy formulation and implementation, and the credibility of the government's commitment to such policies.

[4] Regulatory Quality (RQ) – measures perceptions of the ability of the government to formulate and implement sound policies and regulations that permit and promote private sector development.

[5] Rule of Law (RL) – measures perceptions of the extent to which agents have confidence in and abide by the rules of society, in particular the quality of contract enforcement, property rights, the police, and the courts, as well as the likelihood of crime and violence.

[6] Control of Corruption (CC) – measures perceptions of the extent to which public power is exercised for private gain, including both petty and grand forms of corruption, as well as "capture" of the state by elites and private interests.

Sources: Kaufmann et al. (2010), World Bank.

below Uruguay, faring better in the other dimensions with respect to these two countries, however. In turn, Chile scores below but not too far away from the average of the OECD in five dimensions and would be in a better position than the OECD in regulatory quality according to this index. (See Chapter 7 for comments on the regulatory performance of the Chilean state in concentrated markets.)

The Business and Investment Climate

Another survey, based on perceptions of domestic-firm executives, investors, transnational corporations, and others, was prepared by the Geneva-based World Economic Forum (WEF). The survey seeks to identify "problematic factors" that affect the business and investment climate of countries that compete for foreign investment. As with the World Bank's index, this index is subjective and oriented toward gauging business conditions for the private sector (often large firms and multinationals). In this vein, these factors try to be an implicit guide for deciding which countries present better (or worse) conditions for investing. Table 8.4 gives the results for Argentina, Bolivia, and Chile in 2008.

It is interesting to note that in Argentina, as well as in Bolivia, the instability of public policies is identified by survey respondents as the first obstacle to investment. The second most problematic factor identified for Argentina and Bolivia, associated probably with the instability of public policies, is inflation. The lack of funding (credit), corruption, and employment restrictions are other factors inhibiting investment in Argentina. In Bolivia, political instability (including military coups), government bureaucracy, and corruption appear as problematic factors as well. In Chile, on the contrary, the instability of public policies is not among the five most important obstacles to investment and business. The most problematic factor for private investment identified by respondents is the restrictive employment regulations, followed by "government bureaucracy." It is interesting that this last result is somewhat at odds with the relatively high rating of government effectiveness as noted by the World Bank's index. Other factors identified in the World Economic Forum's index as problematic elements for investors in Chile are a workforce with insufficient education levels, the existence of corruption, and a lack of work ethics. This survey

Table 8.4. *Business and Investment Climate: Argentina, Bolivia, and Chile (WEF, 2008)*

Argentina		Bolivia		Chile	
Problematic Factor	**Score**	**Problematic Factor**	**Score**	**Problematic Factor**	**Score**
1. Instability of Public Policy	22.9	1. Instability of Public Policy	18.2	1. Restrictive Labor Regulations	26
2. Inflation	15.2	2. Inflation	14.1	2. Inefficient Government Bureaucracy	17.6
3. Access to Financing	11.0	3. Instability of Governments/ Coups d'etat	13.4	3. Inadequately Educated Workforce	11.7
4. Corruption	8.6	4. Inefficient Government Bureaucracy	8.8	4. Corruption	6.5
5. Restrictive Labor Regulations	8.4	5. Corruption	7.9	5. Low Work Ethic Workforce	5.2

Note: The information shown comes from the 2008 edition of the Economic Forum survey given to business executives of 134 economies. From a list of 15 factors, the executives chose the 5 more problematic factors in their countries, arranging them from 1 (most problematic) to 5 (least problematic). The final scores were tabulated and adjusted, with rankings based on the answers. Final scores are given in Table 8.4. A higher score means that the factor is more problematic.
Sources: Blanke et al. (2008–9), World Economic Forum.

reveals the importance investors attach to governance in their evaluation of the investment climate, an important variable in determining a country's capacity for economic growth.

Concluding Remarks

This chapter has highlighted the shortcomings and contradictions of the Chilean democracy that emerged after the military regime, along with some positive features of the governance of the country as perceived by the private sector, both national and international. The long transition of the democracy initiated in the early 1990s was surrounded by a series of anomalous features such as the 1980s constitution approved

under the military regime and only partially reformed, a fraction of
the senate appointed and thus not elected by citizens, the powers of
the military-based national security council, the lack of political rights
for Chileans abroad and at home, and the concentration of ownership
of mass media. The nonelected senators and the excessive powers of
the national security council were eliminated by the reforms of 2005,
but other features of an incomplete democracy remain.

In contrast, Chile fares reasonably well according to indexes of governance based on perceptions by national and international private
sectors regarding quality of political institutions, quality of macroeconomic management, effectiveness of regulatory bodies, the rule of law,
and control of corruption when compared with other Latin American
countries and even the OECD. Regrettably, no comparable systematic
survey of "quality of institutions" is applied to noninvestors, workers,
or members of grassroots organizations regarding consumer rights,
respect for workers legislation, information disclosure of companies,
and other similar issues.

These results show that Chile has competent macroeconomic and
other state institutions but within a framework in which the interests
of capital (the private sector) and the economic model take priority
over a more complete and participatory democracy and economy, one
that would give labor and other social movements and political parties
a greater voice and participation in public policies and politics, as well
as respect for consumer and social rights.

9

Summary and Issues for the Future

Introduction

Chile has undergone an economic revolution in the past three decades. This free-market revolution released entrepreneurial energy and a capacity for wealth creation. Nevertheless, as emphasized in this book, the bulk of the newly created wealth tends to go overwhelmingly into the hands of economic elites. As a consequence of this, structural inequality in income and asset distribution is a main feature that characterizes Chilean society today. The middle class and the poor have improved their lot, but they remain disempowered and vulnerable to economic shocks. In retrospect, it is fair to say that the democratic administrations ruling between 1990 and 2009, in spite of their significant achievements of steering a peaceful return to an (incomplete) democracy and maintaining prosperity, ultimately lacked the political capacity and intellectual conviction to turn a model that was yielding good results in the growth and macroeconomic fronts into a more balanced and socially equitable strategy of economic development. The post-Pinochet social-democratic governments focused on reducing income poverty and creating the basic institutions to reduce social risks but were oblivious to growing inequality and concentration of economic power by the elites. The tools employed were increased social expenditure, higher minimum wages, the gradual strengthening of institutions managing social policy, and expanded physical infrastructure in social sectors. In the 2000s, the socialist presidents Lagos and Bachelet shifted the emphasis of policies to social protection and social rights. Partial reforms to the health and pension systems were

149

introduced, and a regressive constitutional education law (LOCE), which came from the last days of the Pinochet regime, was modified under pressure from the student movement. Whatever the merits and good intentions of the partial social reforms of the 2000s, these attempts were in the end of relatively limited impact and constrained by powerful economic elites whose interests could be affected by genuinely equitable and democratic social reforms. The profit motive that dominates the provision of education, health, and pensions for the population was never seriously curtailed by the reforms of the 2000s despite the demands of the mass of beneficiaries for the introduction of new systems for the delivery of social services. The high concentration in the ownership and management of the pension funds of the general population and the private provision of health services were not challenged by these reforms. Boosting effective competition and initiating social controls over the use of the savings of the working and the middle classes for old age were postponed indefinitely. The creation of unemployment insurance was an advancement over a situation of no insurance, but the new system had restricted coverage and excluded employees in both the informal sector and a public sector characterized by increased job insecurity and the widespread use of temporary contracts for public sector employees.

Economic and Developmental Institutions

Chile is now an OECD country. At the same time, however, Chile is an atypical OECD economy in its levels of inequality, the prevalence of the profit motive in the delivery of social services, the limited regulation of oligopolies, and the concentration of economic power in small elites. Chile made good progress in macroeconomic policies but shows an uneven institutional matrix. The central bank and finance ministry are much more influential in defining development priorities and policies than the ministries and agencies in charge of production development, social policy, cultural development, and the protection of the environment. The technocracy of the monetary and fiscal institutions has developed since the early 2000s under socialist presidents, as well as a strict orthodoxy of fiscal rules, inflation targeting, free short-term capital inflows, and floating exchange rates with occasional intervention by the monetary authorities. Another issue is the need to reinforce the ability of regulatory bodies to foster competition and reduce economic concentration in banking, pension-fund management, retail, pharmacies, and health insurance. Consumer protection must also be strengthened in a complex market economy plagued with information asymmetries and the unrelenting search for profits by powerful economic conglomerates. Effective regulation, however, is bound to be difficult. Risks of capture or neutralization of the regulator are always present given the power of the regulated industries, several of them cartelized and employing collusive practices.

Economic Growth

The growth acceleration of the past twenty-five years or so was concentrated mainly in 1986–97, when the economy grew at an average rate of nearly 7.5 percent per year. In the 2000s, however, resuming growth beyond the threshold of 4 to 5 percent per year, on a sustained basis, has been very difficult despite very favorable copper prices, increased fiscal resources, and ample international reserves. Perhaps this trend of growth deceleration is a sign of a certain exhaustion of the Chilean model.

Chilean growth will face various constraints and challenges in the years ahead: the need to be more geographically diversified, to move away from a high reliance on natural resources while reducing the intensity of energy usage, the limits posed by a pattern of growth concentrated in the elites for the expansion of the domestic market and the indebtedness of the working and middle classes, the pace of growth of worker productivity, and other factors. Another dilemma is how to grow the tradable-goods sector given a scenario of a sluggish growth in the advanced economy, volatility, and a loss of external competitiveness owing to an appreciation of the real exchange rate, which hampers the profitability of the nonmineral tradable sector and agricultural exports. A reduction of inequality would be necessary for a growth path more oriented toward the internal market and less sensitive to the cycles of the international economy.

Democracy and Governance

The Chilean democracy that emerged after the military regime was limited by constitutional enclaves and restrictions that ensured the consolidation of the economic model. The Chilean political system is oriented toward protecting the hegemony of the economic elites and the political establishment in face of a potentially empowered citizenship and social movements. The country's constitution makes it very difficult to hold plebiscites and to reform itself and gives absolute primacy to private property and markets over state ownership and social rights. An example of the low priority given to civil and political rights is the fact that Chileans abroad are not allowed to vote in national elections in Chile. In turn, the binomial system ensures the exclusion of non-Concertación left-wing political parties, ecological movements, and ethnic minorities, and grants special privileges to the armed forces in terms of ample budgets, special pension and health systems, and the national security council.

The current institutional matrix – the array of political and economic institutions that define the governance of the country and its political system – in Chile exhibits several contrasts and contradictions. Chile fares reasonably well according to subjective indexes of the private sector that express degrees of contentment (or dissatisfaction) with how well political institutions handle regulatory bodies, the rule of law, and the control of corruption when compared with other Latin American countries and even the OECD. Its democracy, however, shows evident limitations.

New Social Contract: More Political and Economic Democracy

Chile needs a new social contract to marry the dynamism in wealth creation with social equity, effective economic security, and more democracy. The economic elites not only control the bulk of production assets but also promote a conformist culture through their overwhelming control of the mass media. A new social contract for Chile should reduce the large gaps in income, wealth, opportunities, access to social services, and political participation that characterize the current social contract. This requires shifting economic power to the middle class and the working poor through a more active state, effective regulatory policies, a revision of the tax structure, a new deal with multinational corporations in the strategic copper sector that is more favorable to the interests of Chilean state, a deconcentration of the ownership of productive wealth, and the empowering of new social actors (youth, ecological groups, workers and the middle class) who can counter the influence and power of the national and international elites. Assets and credit markets need to reach broader segments of the population, and effective competition policies are needed. The positive behavior of the macro economy, the accumulated savings in the public sector, and the enormous economic surplus capacity (profits) generated in mining at a time of record copper prices, along with high profits in banking, retail, and utilities, almost entirely internalized by a small group of private owners, provide a significant material base for effective social reforms and the improvement of the conditions of the middle class and the poor. The priorities of the Chilean development model must undergo a renewal, moving away from the unwarranted faith in the neoliberal belief that only profits, markets, and narrow economic growth is the magic cure-all for the social and environmental challenges facing Chilean society. The winds of change in economics and public policy and the emergence of broad social movements demanding fairer economic systems and democracy, triggered by the cumulative contradictions of the neoliberal era as well as the financial crisis of 2008–9, are reaching Chile. A more even distribution of income, assets, opportunities, and influence will spur social cohesion and enhance economic democracy.

To achieve these goals and aspirations, interventions in the following areas are needed:

- A priority for society and the state must be set to reduce income and wealth inequality in a reasonable time frame. This should include the redefinition of the development strategy to include broader equity and environmental goals, beyond maximizing GDP per capita, as the overriding criteria for defining economic and social development.
- New policies should incorporate the middle class as a valid beneficiary of social policy in housing, education, health, pensions and other relevant dimensions. Progress in some of these areas was made in the past two decades, but social policy was largely guided by targeting low-income groups and excluding the middle class, not to mention an unjustified faith in the trickle-down theory of aggregate economic growth.

- An effective education reform should be implemented, one oriented to foster social mobility, knowledge acquisition, and the reduction of inequalities. This reform must promote a recovery of good-quality public education, at low cost or for free, to redress the significant imbalances of resources and priorities between public and private schools and should effectively engage students, teachers, and the community at large. The crisis of the university system in Chile, segmented, profit-oriented, expensive, and heterogeneous in quality, is also very apparent.
- Policies to "destratify" access to health care are needed, a feature that the AUGE plan is short in addressing. The health system remains strongly segmented. Only the upper-middle classes and the rich can afford the higher quality of care available in the privately provided social service system, whereas the bulk of the middle class and the poor must receive largely underfunded, lower-quality care in the public system.
- True and full equity must be brought to the social security (pension) system. Although President Bachelet adopted changes to lower the floor of pension contributions to increase affordability, to make coverage "universal," and to correct discrimination against women, the high-fee private capitalization pension system through which a handful of private companies administer the pensions of millions of people remains intact. The vulnerability of the system became apparent when the financial crisis of 2008 reduced the value of pensions in higher-risk financial portfolios. The same holds true for volatility in other episodes of financial crisis and turbulence.
- Bargaining and economic power, which had been severely debilitated during the Pinochet regime and became a bargaining chip for the Concertación government in the transition from the military regime to the democracy, must be returned to labor and employees. The problem of massive youth unemployment, which breeds crime, drugs, and social discontent, must be tackled in an urgent manner.
- Antitrust and nationalization policies must be considered to reduce the concentration of ownership and wealth in economic conglomerates in critical sectors of the economy including the copper sector. This concentration effectively squeezes small and medium-size businesses out of the export markets and privatizes record profits in a society with many unmet social needs.

- The environment and natural resources must be protected. A national copper policy, today non-existing, is needed that reviews and redefine the current conditions such as ownership, royalty and taxation levels, environmental impact, respect for contracts with the state under which foreign companies exploit copper, the main national wealth of Chile, which, according to the current constitution, is owned by the Chilean state. The current passivity of the state should be replaced of an active defense of Chilean natural resource base.

- In line with the previous point, Chile, must define priorities and identify appropriate policy tools for protecting natural resources and the environment considering national interests and sustainability considerations rather than the interests of big national and foreign corporations.

- Finally, Chile needs urgent political reforms and the elaboration, through a democratically elected constitutional assembly, of a new constitution that replaces the neoliberal constitutional chart of 1980. This would be a first step towards the restoration of genuine democracy in Chile. The new constitution should reestablish the priorities of civil, economic, and social rights over markets and profits. In turn, a new constitutional chart should encourage participative democratic processes moving away from the practice of the last three decades of close-doors decision-making in public policy, a practice often favoring the status-quo and the interests of the powerful economic and political elites dominating Chilean society.

References

Acemoglu, D., and J. Robinson (2006), "Persistence of Power, Elites and Institutions," *NBER Working Paper* 12108.

Agostini, C. (2008), La organización industrial del transporte aéreo en Chile, *Revista de Análisis Económico*, vol. 23, no. 1 (June), pp. 35–84.

Alesina, A., and D. Rodrik (1994), "Distributive Politics and Economic Growth," *Quarterly Journal of Economics*, 109 (2): 456–90.

Arendt, H. (1958), *The Human Condition*, University of Chicago Press: Chicago BBC News Report, Tuesday, December 30, 2008, available at www.bbc.co.uk.

Ayyagari, M., T. Beck, and A. Demirguc-Kunt (2005), "Small and Medium Enterprisers across the Globe," (mimeo) World Bank.

Bastías, G., T. Pantoja, T. Leisewitz, and V. Zárate (2008), "Health Care Reform in Chile," *Canadian Medical Association Journal*, vol. 179, no. 12 (December), pp. 1289–92.

Baumol, W., J. Panzar, and R. Willig (1988), *Contestable Markets and the Theory of Industry Structure*, Harcourt Brace Jovanovich: San Diego.

Bell, D. (1976), *The Cultural Contradictions of Capitalism*, Basic Books: New York.

Benitez, J., y P. Rosas, editores (2009), *La Republica Inconclusa: Una Nueva Constitución Para el Bicentenario*, Editorial Arcis, Santiago, Chile.

Bitar, S. (1979), *Transición, Socialismo y Democracia*, Siglo Veintiuno Editores: Mexico City.

Blanchard, O., G. Dell Ariccia, and P. Mauro (2010), "Rethinking Macroeconomic Policy," *IMF Staff Position Note* February, SPN/10/03.

Bowen, G. L. (2006), "United States Policy toward Chile", Departments of Political Science and International Relations, Mary Baldwin College, VA.

CASEN Survey, various years, Planning Ministry, Government of Chile.

Corbo, V., and A. Solimano (1991), "Chile's Experience with Stabilization Revisited," in M. Bruno, S. Fischer, E. Helpman, N. Liviatan, with L. Meridor, editors, *Lessons of Economic Stabilization and Its Aftermath*, MIT Press: Cambridge, MA.

Davies, J. (2008), *Personal Wealth from a Global Perspective*, Oxford University Press.

Davies, J., S. Sandstrom, A. Shorrocks, and E. N. Wolff (2006), "The World Distribution of Household Wealth," UNU-WIDER: Helsinki, available at: www.iariw.org/papers/2006/davies.pdf

De Gregorio, J. (2004), "Economic Growth in Chile: Evidence, Sources and Prospects," *Central Bank Working Paper* 298, Central Bank of Chile: Santiago de Chile.

De Gregorio, J., and A. Tokman (2004), "Overcoming Fear of Floating: Exchange Rate Policies in Chile," *Central Bank Working Paper* 302, Central Bank of Chile: Santiago de Chile.

Díaz, J., R. Lüders, and G. Wagner (2007), "Economía Chilena 1810–2000: Producto Total y Sectorial, Una Nueva Mirada," *Documento de Trabajo* 315, Instituto de Economía, Pontificia Universidad Católica de Chile: Santiago de Chile.

Dixit, A. (1996), *The Making of Economic Policy: A Transaction-Cost Politics Approach*, MIT Press: Cambridge, MA.

Edwards, S., and A. Edwards (1987), *Monetarism and Liberalization: The Chilean Experiment*, Ballinger Publishing: Cambridge, MA.

Fazio, H. (2005), *Mapa de la Extrema Riqueza al año 2005*, LOM Ediciones, Colección Ciencias Sociales: Santiago de Chile.

Ffrench-Davis, R. (2002), *Economic Reforms in Chile: From Dictatorship to Democracy*, University of Michigan Press: Ann Arbor, MI.

(1973), *Políticas Económicas en Chile 1950–70*, Ediciones Nueva Universidad: Santiago de Chile.

Foley, D. (2006), *Adam's Fallacy: A Guide to Economic Theology*, Belknap Press of Harvard University Press.

Forbes magazine (2011), "The World's Richest People: World's Billionaires," online edition, available at: www.forbes.com.

Forgacs, D. (1988), *An Antonio Gramsci Reader: Selected Writings, 1916–1935*, Lawrence and Wishart: London.

Foxley, A. (1983), *Latin American Experiments in Neo-Conservative Economics*, University of California Press: Berkeley.

Fuentes, R., M. Larraín, and K. Schmidt-Hebbel (2006), "Sources of Growth and Behaviour of the TFP in Chile," *Cuadernos de Economía*, 43 (May), 113–42.

Gomez-Leyton, J. (2010), *Política, Democracia y Ciudadanía en una sociedad neoliberal (Chile: 1990–2010)*, Editorial ARCIS/PROSPAL/CLACSO: Santiago de Chile.

Grez, S. (2009), "La Ausencia de un Poder Constituyente Democrático en la Historia de Chile," en Le Monde Diplomatique, *Asamblea Constituyente, Nueva Constitución*, pp. 35–58, A. Ramis, J, Guzmán, R. Garretón and S. Grez, contributors, Editorial Aun Creemos en los Sueños, Santiago, Chile.

Harvey, D. (2010), *The Enigma of Capital and the Crises of Capitalism*, Profile Books, Great Britain.

Hayner, P. (2001), *Unspeakable Truths: Confronting State Terror and Atrocity*, Routledge: New York, NY.

Hirschman A. (1982), *Shifting Involvements. Private Interest and Public Action*, Princeton University Press: Princeton, NJ.

Hobsbawm, E. (2011), *How to Change the World: Tales of Marx and Marxism*, Little, Brown, Great Britain.

Infante, A., and G. Paraje (2010), "Reforma de Salud. Garantías Exigibles Como Derecho Ciudadano," chapter 2 in O. Larrañaga and D. Contreras, editors (2010), *Las Nuevas Políticas de Protección Social en Chile*, PNUD: Santiago de Chile.

Infante, R. (2011), "El Sector Informal en Chile," chapter 2 in *Chile: El Impacto del Mercado Laboral en el Bienestar de las Personas*, Organizacion Internacional del Trabajo, Santiago de Chile.

Infante, R., and O. Sunkel (2009), "Chile: hacia un desarrollo inclusive," *Revista CEPAL*, no. 97, April, pp. 135–54.

Infante, R., and G., Sunkel (2004), *Chile: Trabajo decente y calidad de vida familiar, 1990–2000*, Organizacion Internacional del Trabajo, Santiago de Chile.

Jackson, T. (2009), *Prosperity without Growth: Economics for a Finite Planet*, EarthScan: London and Washington DC.

Kaletsky, A. (2010), *Capitalism 4.0: The Birth of a New Economy*, Bloomsburry: London, Berlin and New York.

Kaufmann, D., A. Kraay, and M. Mastruzzi (2010), "The Worldwide Governance Indicators: Methodology and Analytical Issues," *Policy Research Working Paper Series* 5430, World Bank: Washington, DC.

Kornbluh, P. (2004), *Pinochet: Los archivos secretos*, Memoria critica, Spain.

Larrañaga, O., and D. Contreras, editors (2010), *Las Nuevas Políticas de Protección Social en Chile*, PNUD: Santiago de Chile.

Larrain, F. (2008), "Cuatro Millones de Pobres en Chile: Actualizando la Línea de Pobreza en Chile," *Estudios Públicos*, vol. 109, Santiago de Chile.

Larraín, F., and P. Meller (1990), "*La Experiencia Socialista-Populista Chilena: La Unidad Popular, 1970–73*," Colección de Estudios CIEPLAN, CIEPLAN: Santiago de Chile.

Lopez, R., and S. Miller (2008), "Chile: The Unbearable Burden of Inequality," *World Development*, 26 (12): 2679–95.

Maldonado, R. (comp.) (1993), "*Pedro Vuskovic, Obras Escogidas sobre Chile 1964–1992*," Colección Chile en el Siglo XX, Ediciones Centro de Estudios Políticos Latinoamericanos Simón Bolívar: Santiago de Chile.

Marglin, S. (2008), *The Dismal Science: How Thinking Like an Economist Undermines Community*, Harvard University Press: Cambridge, MA.

Marx, K. (1848 [1979]), *The Communist Manifesto*, Penguin books: London.

Meller, P. (1997), *Un Siglo de Economía Política Chilena: 1890–1990*, Editorial Andrés Bello: Santiago de Chile.

Mönckeberg, M. (2009), *Los Magnates de la Prensa*, Editorial Debate: Santiago de Chile.

North, D. (1991), "Institutions, Transaction Costs, and the Rise of Merchant Empires," chapter 1 in J. Tracy, editor, *The Political Economy of Merchant Empires*, Cambridge University Press: Cambridge, New York.

NotiSur (2004), "Chile: Congress Reforms Pinochet-era Constitution," *NotiSur – South American Political and Economic Affairs*, October 22, 2004.

Ocular Surgery News (1999), "Chile's Diversified Health System Tested by Economic, Demographic Changes," *Ocular Surgery News*, June 1, 1999, available at http://www.osnsupersite.com/view.aspx?rid=15008.

OECD and ECLAC (2005), *Evaluaciones de desempeño ambiental: Chile*, CEPAL: Santiago de Chile.

OECD-WB (2009), *Reviews of National Policies for Education: Tertiary Education in Chile*, OECD publishing: Paris.

Pastor, D. (2004), "Origins of the Chilean Binominal Election System," *Revista de Ciencia Política*, vol. 24, no. 1, pp. 38–57.

Polanyi, K. (1944), *The Great Transformation: Economic and Political Origins of Our Time*, Rinehart: New York.

Quiggin, J. (2010), *Zombie Economics: How Dead Ideas Still Walk Among Us*, Princeton University Press: Princeton, NJ, and Oxford, UK.

Ramos, J., and C. Acero (2010), "El Seguro de Desempleo," cap. 3 en Larrañaga, O. and D. Contreras, editores (2010), *Las Nuevas Políticas de Protección Social en Chile*, PNUD: Santiago de Chile.

Riesco, M. (2008), *Cambios en el Modelo Social Chileno*, CENDA: Santiago de Chile.

Salazar, G. (2009), *Del Poder Constituyente de Asalariados e Intelectuales (Chile, Siglos XX y XXI)*, Lom Ediciones, Historia: Santiago de Chile.

Sen, A. (2009), *The Idea of Justice*, Harvard University Press: Cambridge, MA.

Sercotec (2005), "La Situación de la Micro y Pequeña Empresa en Chile," Program Chile Emprende, Sercotev, Government of Chile.

Siavelis, P. (2000), *The President and Congress in Post-Authoritarian Chile: Institutional Constraints to Democratic Consolidation*, Pennsylvania State University Press: University Park, PA.

SII (Chilean Customs Office and Internal Revenue Service) (2003), SII Web site, available at www.sii.cl.

Smith, A. (1759 [2007]), *The Theory of Moral Sentiments*, Standard Publications, Incorporated O Book Jungle.

Solimano, A. (2010a), "How Relevant Is IMF Research on Macro-Financial Linkages to Reduce the Frequency of Financial Crisis and Recessions in the World Economy? An Overview," paper prepared for the Independent Evaluation Office of the IMF.

(2010b), *International Migration in the Age of Crisis and Globalization*, Cambridge University Press.

(2009), "Three Decades of Neoliberal Economics in Chile: Achievements, Failures and Dilemmas," UNU-WIDER Research Paper no. 2009/37 (June).

(2008), "The Middle Class and the Development Process," chapter 2 in A. Estache and D. Leipziger, editors, *Stuck in the Middle: Is Fiscal Policy Failing the Middle Class?*, Brookings Institution.

(2007), "Sobre la Reproducción de la Desigualdad en Chile: Concentración de Activos, Estructura Productiva y Matriz Institucional," *CIGLOB Working Paper* 01, International Center for Globalization and Development: Santiago de Chile.

(2006), *Vanishing Growth in Latin America: The Late Twentieth Century Experience*, Edward Elgar Publishing: United Kingdom.

(2005), *Political Crises, Social Conflict and Economic Development: The Political Economy of the Andean Region*, Edward Elgar Publishing: United Kingdom.

(1999), "The Chilean Economy in the 1990s: On a Golden Age and Beyond," in L. Taylor, editor, *After Neoliberalism: What Next for Latin America?*, University of Michigan Press: Chicago.

Solimano, A., editor (1998), *Social Inequality: Values, Growth and the State*, University of Michigan Press: Chicago.

Solimano, A. (1993), "Chile," in L. Taylor, editor, *The Rocky Road to Reform: Adjustment, Income Distribution and Growth in the Developing World*, MIT Press: Cambridge, MA.

Solimano, A., and M. Gutierrez (2009), "Savings, Investment and Capital Accumulation," chapter 6, in A. Dutt and J. Ross, editors, *Handbook of International Development*, vol. I, Edward Elgar Publishers.

Solimano, A., and M. Pollack (2007), *La Mesa Coja: Prosperidad y Desigualdad en el Chile Democrático*, CIGLOB Ediciones: Santiago de Chile.

Solimano, A., and A. Torche (2008), "La Distribución del Ingreso en Chile 1987–2006: Análisis y Consideraciones de Política," *Central Bank of Chile Working Papers*, no. 480, Banco Central de Chile: Santiago de Chile.

(2007), "La Distribución del Ingreso en Chile 1987–2006: Análisis y Consideraciones de Política," *CIGLOB Working Paper 04*, International Center for Globalization and Development: Santiago de Chile.

Solimano, A., E. Aninat, and N. Birdsall, editors (2000), *Distributive Justice and Economic Development: The Case of Chile and Developing Countries*, University of Michigan Press, Chicago.

Solimano, A., M. Pollack, U. Weiner, and J. Wurgaft (2007), "Micro Empresas, PyMES y. Desarrollo Económico: Chile y la Experiencia Internacional," *CIGLOB Working Paper* no. 03, International Center for Globalization and Development: Santiago de Chile.

South Pacific Applied Geosciences Commission (SOPAC) and United Nations Environmental Programme (UNEP) (2005), "Building Resilience in SIDS: The Environmental Vulnerability Index," available at www.vulnerabilityindex.net.

Stiglitz, J., and A. Weiss (1981), "Credit Rationing in Markets with Imperfect Information," *American Economic Review*, vol. 71, no. 3 (June), pp. 393–410.

Stockholm International Peace Research Institute (SIPRI) (2011), online database at www.sipri.org

Sunkel, O. (1994), "La crisis social de América Latina: Una perspectiva neoestructuralista," in C. Contreras, editor, *El desarrollo social, tarea de todos:* Comisión Sudamericana de Paz, Seguridad y Democracia.

United Nations, Public Administration Network (2010), "E-Government Survey 2010: Leveraging E-government at a Time of Financial and Economic Crisis," online version at www.unpan.org.

Vergara R. (2004), "Taxation and Private Investment: Evidence for Chile," *Documento de trabajo* N° 268, pp. 1–23, Instituto de Economía, Pontificia Universidad Católica de Chile.

Weber, M. (1905 [2001]), *The Protestant Ethic and the Spirit of Capitalism*, Routledge: New York.

Wright-Mills, C. (1956 [2000]), *The Power Elite*, Oxford University Press: New York.

Wolff, J. (2003), *Why Read Marx Today?*, Oxford University Press: Oxford.

World Bank (2008), *World Development Report 2009*, World Bank: Washington.

World Economic Forum (2011), "The Global Information Technology Report 2010–2011: Transformations 2.0," online version at www.weforum.org.

(2010), "The Global Gender Gap Report 2010," online version at www.weforum.org.

Yale Center for Environmental Law and Policy (YCELP) and Center for International Earth Science Information Network (CIESIN) (2005), "2005 Environmental Sustainability Index: Benchmarking National Environmental Stewardship," available at http://sedac.ciesin.columbia.edu/es/esi/.

Index

AFP. *See* Pension Fund Administrators
Agrarian reform, 19, 21
Aggregate demand, 21, 25–26, 54–56, 65
Agricultural sector, 3, 67, 131–132, 151
Alianza por Chile, 37, 139
Allende, Salvador, 20–23, 52, 115, 117, 135
APEC. *See* Asia-Pacific Economic Cooperation
Argentina, 1, 4, 58–59, 141, 144, 146
Armed forces, 10, 16–17, 22–23, 30, 36–37, 109, 136, 138, 140
Asian financial crisis. *See* financial crisis
Asia-Pacific Economic Cooperation, 31, 98
Assets ownership. *See* Concentration
AUGE plan, 32, 95, 107–110
Authoritarian regime. *See* Military regime
Aylwin, Patricio, 24, 29–31, 63, 69–71, 95–98, 115

Bachelet, Michelle, 2, 6, 32, 63–65, 69–72, 95–98, 104, 110, 113, 115, 149
Balance of payments, 20, 33, 56, 71
Balanced budget rule. *See* Fiscal rule
Banking sector, 21, 26–28, 85, 125–127, 131, 136, *See also* Central Bank of Chile
Bell, Daniel, 43, 45
Billionaires. *See Forbes* ranking
Binomial system, 11, 137, 139, 152
Bolivia, 141, 144, 146
Boom in copper price. *See* Copper price

Brazil, 8, 58–59, 100, 141, 144
Bureaucracy, 144–147

Capital inflows, 22, 25, 33, 66, 146
    short-term tax on, 31, 32, 62, 64, 69
Capital markets, 4, 55
Capital-labor power balance, 30, 42, 75, 83–86, 115, 119, 136, 153–154
CASEN survey, 76–78, 129–130
Catholic Church. *See* Church
Central Bank of Chile, 18, 26, 32, 61–62, 66, 68–69
Centralism, 11, 35, 132–134
Chicago boys, 8, 25
China, 1, 5, 58–59, 69
Christian Democrats, 19, 20, 24, 31, 75
Church, 35, 41
Civil society. *See* Social movements
Coalicion por el Cambio. See Alianza por Chile
CODELCO. *See Corporación Nacional del Cobre*
Collective bargaining. *See* Labor unions
Colombia, 58, 142
Commodities, 5, 71, *See also* Copper price, Natural resources
Communist party of Chile, 19, 139
Competitiveness, 66–67, 151,
    See also Exports
Concentration
    of economic power, 20–21, 84–86, 120–122
    geographic, 4, 132–134
    market, 124–134, 150

163

Concertación, 9, 29–34, 37, 43, 48, 61, 63, 69–72, 75, 84, 87, 139
Conglomerate. *See* holdings
Congress, 10–11, 17–18, 29, 37, 139
Constitution, 10, 16–18, 29, 34–38, 135, 137–140, 155
Constitutional reform, 11, 32, 37, 137–138
Construction industry, 6, 99, 131
Contraction. *See* Economic crisis
Copper industry. *See* Mining industry
Copper price, 5, 64
  boom in, 33, 71
Corporación Nacional del Cobre, 5, 10, 121, 138
Corporate income tax. *See* Tax
Corruption, 24, 144–147
Counter-cyclical policies, 6, 33, 65,
  See also Fiscal rule
Coup d'état, 8, 18, 22, 36, 47, 103, 116–117, 135
Credit
  access to, 65, 85, 128–129, 153
  external, 22, 25
Culture, 39–49
Current account, 26, 33, 53, 63, 70,
  See also Deficit

Davies, James, 56
De Gregorio, José, 54, 68
Debt
  public, 31, 65
  external, 26, 31
Defense spending. *See* Military
  expenditures
Deficit
  current account, 26, 56, 61, 71
  fiscal, 20, 21, *See also* Fiscal balance
Deflation, 68
Democracy, 9, 10, 16–19, 84–85, 140–143, 152–153
  restoration of, 2, 24, 29–30, 38, 47, 50, 75, 93, 135–140
Diaz, José, 52–53, 57
Dictatorship. *See* Military regime

Earthquake of 2010, 79, 86
Economic and Social Stabilization Fund, 6, 34, 65
Economic crisis, 6, 25–28, 52, 55, 58, 61, 79, 116, *See also* financial crisis
Economic growth. *See* GDP growth

Economic miracle of Chile, 50–58
Education, 44–45, 76, 85–86, 93–94, 98, 154
  public, 101, 106–107
  pre-schooling, 99, 106
  private, 94, 101–102, 106–107, 121–122
  reforms, 14, 31, 76, 100–106, 122
  tertiary, 101, 103, 106–107
Electoral participation, 11, 29,
  See also Political participation
Electoral system. *See* Binomial system
Elites, 2, 8, 21, 22, 34, 81–82, 120–124, 149–150
Energy consumption, 60
Energy generation, 60
Environment, 5, 7, 58, 60–61, 122, 150, 155
Environmental groups, 7, 32, 139
Environmental policies, 98
Ethics, 39–40, *See also* Individualism
European Union, 5
Exchange rate
  regime, 27, 32, 62, 64, 66–68, 151
  intervention, 25, 27, 63, 67–68
Exports, 25, 53, 56, 59, 131–132, 151
  copper, 5
External borrowing. *See* Credit
External shocks, 26, 66, 68–69, 71–72, 79, 149

Federal Reserve of United States of
  America, 62
Financial crisis, 26, 31, 52
  of 2008–2009, 1, 6, 33, 65, 79, 116, 153,
  See also Economic crisis
Financial markets liberalization.
  See Neoliberal reforms
Financial sector. *See* Banking sector
Fiscal balance, 6, 20, 21, 26, 33, 53, 56, 63, 65, 70–71
Fiscal rule, 32, 62–65, 71
FONASA. *See* Fondo Nacional de Salud
Fondo Nacional de Salud, 108–110
Forbes ranking, 8, 48, 122–124
Forestry sector, 3, 125–127
Free market, 1, 8, 24, 39–41, 120–121, 136, 149, *See also* Neoliberal reforms
Free press, 47–48, 137, 144–145
Free-trade agreements (FTA), 5, 31
Frei Ruiz-Tagle, Eduardo, 24, 31, 63, 69–71, 95–98
Friedman, Milton, 8, 25, 121

GDP growth, 2, 20, 25, 26, 33, 50–58, 69–72, 82–84, 146–147, 151
  golden years of Chilean, 50–58
  sustainability of, 58–61
  volatility of, 54
GDP per capita, 4, 56
Gender gap, 7, 31–32, 113
GINI coefficient. *See* Income inequality
Globalization, 50–51, 85
Government quality. *See* Bureaucracy
Gramsci, Antonio, 42, 45

Health, 32, 94, 107–110, 125–127, 154,
  See also Fondo Nacional de Salud,
  Instituciones de Salud Previsional
HHI index, 124–127
Higher education. *See* Education
Hirschman, Albert, 46–47
Holdings, 11, 28, 120–121
Housing policies, 99
Human rights, 22–23, 30, 136

Imports
Income inequality, 2, 8, 34, 44, 56, 74–76, 78–88, 94–95, 105, 120–124, 128
Income per capita. *See* GDP per capita
India, 58–59, 69
Individualism, 39–40
Inflation, 20, 21, 25–26, 31–32, 53, 56, 61, 63, 68–71, 117, 146
Inflation targeting, 13, 61–63, 69–71
Informal sector, 114–115
Infrastructure, 30–31, 32, 98
Instituciones de Salud Previsional, 86, 107–110, 125–127
Institutions. *See* Bureaucracy
International aid, 22
International comparisons, 4, 7, 58, 80, 89–92, 140–147
International Monetary Fund, 27
International rankings. *See* International comparisons
International reserves, 26, 151
Investment, 6, 26, 30, 53–55, 144, 146, *See also* Aggregate demand
Invisible hand, 41
ISAPRES. *See Instituciones de Salud Previsional*

Japan, 5
Judiciary, 36

Labor market, 114–119, 127–134
  legislation, 36, 94, 115, 117–118
Labor unions, 11, 20, 30, 35, 39, 85, 87, 115–118, 136
Lagos, Ricardo, 31–32, 38, 63, 69–72, 95–98, 107, 115, 137, 149
Larraín, Felipe, 7, 20, 57, 77–78
Latin America, 1, 8–10, 20, 64, 80, 86, 108, 135, 140–147
  and the Caribbean (LAC), 4, 7, 58, 78
Lüders, Rolf, 52–53, 57

Macroeconomic policies, 30–32, 61–62, 65, 69–72
Macroeconomic stability, 54, 61
Market fundamentalism.
  See Neoliberalism
Marx, Karl, 42, 45, 87
Mass media, 11, 41, 47, 121
Mercado Común del Sur, 31, 98
MERCOSUR. *See Mercado Común del Sur*
Mexico, 31, 58, 100
Middle-income class, 6, 9, 11, 19, 32, 34, 44, 56, 95, 128, 149, *See also* Working class
Military coup of 1973, *See* Coup d'état
Military expenditures, 10, 138
Military regime, 8, 10–11, 22–24, 30, 36–37, 39, 43, 47, 75–76, 87, 94, 103–104, 106–107, 109, 112, 117–118, 135–143
Minimum wage, 30, 31, 94–96, 98, 149
Mining industry, 3, 5, 19, 21, 125–127, 131, 155
Monetary policy, 61–62, 64, 66, 68–69, 150

National Copper Corporation of Chile.
  See CorporaciónNacional del Cobre
National savings, 53, 55–56, 83, 153
Nationalization, 21
Natural resources, 3, 4, 58–60, 74, 151–155
Neoclassical economics, 39–41, 136
Neoliberal reforms, 8, 24–25, 28, 44, 50, 52
Neoliberalism, 1, 9, 24, 30, 32–33, 36, 69, 84–85, 87, 120–122, 136
Newspapers, 11, 47–48, 121
Nixon, Richard, 21, 22, 75
Nominal exchange rate. *See* Exchange rate
Non-elected senators, 37, 139–140

OECD. *See* Organization for Economic Co-operation and Development
Organization for Economic Co-operation and Development, 2, 8, 51, 86, 89, 100, 145–146, 150, 152

Parliament. *See* Congress
Penguins' revolution, 104–105
Pension health institutions. *See Instituciones de Salud Previsional*
Pension system
administrators. *See* Pension Fund Administrators
privatization, 27, 95, 138
reform, 6, 33, 76, 110, 112–114, 126
Pension Fund Administrators, 6, 86, 110, 112–114, 125–127
Peru, 58, 141
Pinochet, Augusto, 1, 8, 22–24, 29–30, 36, 44, 50, 52, 75, 87, 94, 109, 117–118, 135–140
Piñera, Sebastin, 10, 43, 84, 117, 123–124, 138
Plebiscite, 23, 29, 36, 135, 137, 139, 152
Polanyi, Karl, 43–45, 49, 136
Political crisis, 140–143, *See also* Coup d'état
Political participation, 11, 20, 46–47, 136–137, *See also* Electoral participation
Pollack, Molly, 64
Popular Unity. *See Unidad Popular*
Poverty, 4, 6–7, 27, 34, 57, 75–79, 82–83, 93, 95–96, 99–100
extreme, 6–7, 77
line, 77–79
Pre-schooling education. *See* Education
Primary education. *See* Education
Private capitalization system. *See* Pension system
Private education. *See* Education
Privatization, 1, 25, 27, 31, 44, 48, 94, *See also* Neoliberal reforms
Productive structure, 127–134
Property rights, 137, 144–147, 152
Public debt. *See* Debt
Public education. *See* Education

R&D. *See* Research and Development
Reagan, Ronald, 1, 8
Real exchange rate. *See* Exchange rate

Real wages. *See* Wages
Recession. *See* Economic crisis
Redistribution policies, 20, 75, 84, 93
Religion. *See* Church
Repression. *See* Human rights
Research and Development, 7
Richer class. *See* Upper class
Rule of Law. *See* Property rights

Salaries. *See* Wages
Salazar, Gabriel, 16, 135
Secondary education. *See* Education
Senate, 37, 138–140
Services industry, 3, 120, 131
Small and medium enterprises, 6, 7, 114–115, 119, 121, 127–134
SME. *See* Small and medium enterprises
Smith, Adam, 41
Social cohesion, 9, 30, 45, 153
Social conflict, 44–45, 83, 104–105
Social movements, 20, 29, 33, 39, 45, 104–105, 122, 136, 141, 148, 153
Social policies. *See* Education, Health, and Pension system
Social protection, 34, 39, 44, 76, 87, 93, 99–118, 149
Social reforms, 6, 9, 19–20, 30, 33, 75–76, 95–119, 149–150
Socialism, 20, 31
Socialist Party, 20, 24, 31–32, 75
Solimano, Andrés, 26–27, 54–56, 61, 64, 82–84, 86, 97, 114, 120, 129, 141–142
Sovereign wealth fund. *See* Economic and Social Stabilization Fund
State-owned enterprises, 123, *See also Corporación Nacional del Cobre*
Structural surplus rule. *See* Fiscal rule
Subsidies, 30, 80, 98, 104, 106, 113
Super-rich, 122–124, *See also Forbes* Ranking

Tax, 5, 64, 86, 89–92, 95, 152, 155
reforms, 30, 110, *See also* Capital inflows
Television, 11, 48, 121
Terms of trade, 33, 53, 55, 64, 66, 70–71
Tertiary education. *See* Education
Thatcher, Margaret, 1, 8, 24
Total factor productivity, 53, 56, 70
Trade balance. *See* Current account

Trade liberalization, 25, 55
Trade unions. *See* Labor unions

Unemployment, 27, 53, 61, 70–71, 87, 93, 114
Unemployment insurance, 76, 95, 97, 115–116
Unidad Popular, 20–21
Unionization. *See* Labor unions
United Kingdom, 24, 71
United States government, 8, 19, 21, 71, 75
United States of America, 5, 8, 18, 44, 116, 122, 125–126
University of Chicago, 8, 24
Upper class, 4, 81–82, 120–124
Urban area, 3–4, 61, 94

Value Added Tax. *See* Tax

Wages, 21, 27, 44, 53, 61, 69–71, 114–117
Wagner, Gert, 52–53, 57
Washington Consensus, 9, 61, 78, 85, 94–95
Wealth inequality, 56, 74, 120–124, 128, *See also* Income inequality
Weber, Max, 42
Working class, 4, 19, 30, 32, 87, 128, 134, 150–152, *See also* Middle-income class
World Bank, 22, 27, 144, 146
World Economic Forum, 7, 146–147
World Trade Organization, 31, 98